First World War
and Army of Occupation
War Diary
France, Belgium and Germany

5 CAVALRY DIVISION
Headquarters, Branches and Services
Royal Army Medical Corps
Assistant Director Medical Services
1 January 1917 - 31 January 1918

WO95/1162/3

The Naval & Military Press Ltd
www.nmarchive.com
Published in association with The National Archives

Published by

The Naval & Military Press Ltd

Unit 10 Ridgewood Industrial Park,
Uckfield, East Sussex,
TN22 5QE England
Tel: +44 (0) 1825 749494

www.naval-military-press.com
www.nmarchive.com

This diary has been reprinted in facsimile from the original. Any imperfections are inevitably reproduced and the quality may fall short of modern type and cartographic standards.

© **Crown Copyright**
Images reproduced by permission of The National Archives, London, England, 2015.

Contents

Document type	Place/Title	Date From	Date To
Heading	WO95/1162/3		
Heading	Asst Dir Medical Services Jan 1917-Jan 1918		
Heading	War Diary of A.D.M.S. 5th Cavalry Division from 1st January 1917 to 31st January 1917		
War Diary	Dargnies	01/01/1917	31/01/1917
Heading	A.D.M.S. 5th Cavalry Division		
War Diary	Dargnies	01/02/1917	28/02/1917
Heading	A.D.M.S. 5th Can Div		
War Diary	Dargnies	01/03/1917	23/03/1917
War Diary	Peronne	23/03/1917	29/03/1917
War Diary	Villers-Bretonneux	30/03/1917	31/03/1917
Heading	A.D.M.S. 5th Can Div		
War Diary	Villers Bretonneux	01/04/1917	13/04/1917
War Diary	Guizancourt	14/04/1917	30/04/1917
Heading	A.D.M.S. 5th Cav Div		
War Diary	Guizancourt	01/05/1917	14/05/1917
War Diary	Nobescourt Farm	15/05/1917	31/05/1917
Miscellaneous	G.O.C. Sec'bad Cavalry Brigade	13/05/1917	13/05/1917
Miscellaneous	G.O.C. Sec'bad Cavalry Brigade.	14/05/1917	14/05/1917
Miscellaneous	Routine Orders (Medical) by Brevet-Colonel. A.J. Macnab., F.R.C.S., I,M,S, A.D.M.S. 5th Cavalry Division.	11/05/1917	11/05/1917
Miscellaneous	Routine Orders (Medical) by Brevet-Colonel. A.J. Macnab., F.R.C.S., I,M,S, A.D.M.S. 5th Cavalry Division.	21/05/1917	21/05/1917
Miscellaneous	Routine Orders (Medical) by Brevet-Colonel. A.J. Macnab., F.R.C.S., I,M,S, A.D.M.S. 5th Cavalry Division.	23/05/1917	23/05/1917
War Diary	Nobescourt Farm	01/06/1917	30/06/1917
Operation(al) Order(s)	5th Cavalry Division Operation Order (Medical) No. 6	02/06/1917	02/06/1917
Miscellaneous	General Officer Commanding Ambala Cavalry Brigade.	02/06/1917	02/06/1917
Operation(al) Order(s)	5th Cavalry Division. Operation Order (Medical) No. 7	12/06/1917	12/06/1917
Heading	A.D.M.S. 5th Cav Division		
Miscellaneous	G.O.C. Sec"Bad Cavalry Brigade	21/06/1917	21/06/1917
Heading	A.D.M.S. 5th Cav Div		
War Diary	Nobescourt Farm	01/07/1917	09/07/1917
War Diary	Bouvincourt	10/07/1917	13/07/1917
War Diary	St Pol	16/07/1917	29/07/1917
War Diary	Heuchin	31/07/1917	31/07/1917
Heading	A.D.M.S. 5th Cav Div		
Miscellaneous			
War Diary	Heuchin	01/08/1917	31/08/1917
Heading	A.D.M.S. 5th Cav Div		
War Diary	Heuchin	01/09/1917	30/09/1917
Heading	A.D.M.S. 6th Cav Div		
War Diary	Heuchin	01/10/1917	07/10/1917
War Diary	Poperinghe	08/10/1917	14/10/1917
War Diary	Renescure	14/10/1917	15/10/1917
War Diary	Fressin	16/10/1917	31/10/1917
Miscellaneous	Admissions		

Miscellaneous	Statement Showing number of cases of Preventable Diseases admitted to Cavalry Field Ambulances during the month of October 1917.		
Heading	A.D.M.S. 5th Cav Div		
War Diary	Fressin	01/11/1917	09/11/1917
War Diary	Outrebois	10/11/1917	10/11/1917
War Diary	Querrieu	11/11/1917	11/11/1917
War Diary	Bouvincourt	12/11/1917	19/11/1917
War Diary	Fins	19/11/1917	20/11/1917
War Diary	NE of villers-Plouicw	20/11/1917	21/11/1917
War Diary	N.E. of Villers-Plouica	21/11/1917	21/11/1917
War Diary	Equancourt	22/11/1917	22/11/1917
War Diary	Suzanne	23/11/1917	23/11/1917
War Diary	Monchy La Gache	27/11/1917	28/11/1917
War Diary	Monchy-La-Gache	28/11/1917	29/11/1917
War Diary	R 5a West of Epehy	30/11/1917	30/11/1917
Operation(al) Order(s)	5th Cavalry Division. Operation Order (Medical) No. 11	08/11/1917	08/11/1917
Operation(al) Order(s)	5th Cavalry Division. Operation Order (Medical) No. 12	18/11/1917	18/11/1917
Miscellaneous	Appendix "A"		
Miscellaneous	General Staff, 5th Cavalry Division. No. 5812/17	28/11/1917	28/11/1917
Miscellaneous	D.D.M.S. Cavalry Corps. No. 518/M.	24/11/1917	24/11/1917
Heading	A.D.M.P. 5th Cav Div Dec 1917		
War Diary	R 5 a Two Trees West of Epeny	01/12/1917	02/12/1917
War Diary	Longavesnes	03/12/1917	07/12/1917
War Diary	Monchy La Gache	08/12/1917	19/01/1918
War Diary	Monchy	19/01/1918	26/01/1918
War Diary	Bouvincourt	27/01/1918	31/01/1918
Operation(al) Order(s)	5th Cavalry Division. Operation Order (Medical) No. 14	24/01/1918	24/01/1918
Operation(al) Order(s)	5th Cavalry Division. Operation Order (Medical) No. 15	26/01/1918	26/01/1918
Miscellaneous	Statement showing number of admissions to Cavalry Field Ambulance evacuations, transfers to Rest Stations, and number returned to duty during the month of January 1918.		
Heading	Secunderabad Ind Cav F A Jan 1918		

WO 95/1162/3

1917-1918
5TH CAVALRY DIVISION

ASST DIR. MEDICAL SERVICES

JAN 1917 - JAN 1918

SERIAL NO. 8.

COMMITTEE FOR THE
MEDICAL HISTORY OF THE WAR
Date 23 APR. 1917

Confidential
War Diary
of

A.D.M.S., 5th CAVALRY DIVISION.

FROM 1st January 1917 TO 31st January 1917

Army Form C. 2118.

WAR DIARY
or
INTELLIGENCE SUMMARY
(Erase heading not required.)

Vol XXVI 1st 16 31st Jan 1914

ADW&S 8th Bn [illegible]

Place	Date	Hour	Summary of Events and Information	Remarks and references to Appendices
DARRNES	Jan 1		Personnel to Divisional Ammunition Column open their December Parties trained: 3 plat / comm. Strength 2384 Rations trained: 25 plat / comm. Strength 1727	
			Personnel to training Parties trained: 10 plat / comm. Ration trained: 2 per comm.	
"	Jan 3rd		Visits 2nd & 3rd Army Hdqrs	
"	Jan 4th		Started G.S.O.I; At present field exercise carried out by Lt Col A.N. FLEMING, & men in company thrilled into a new Estab. absorption by Reynolds & Pack howitzer Sections. Received & noted on a Scheme for a Combined Pack transport Section & Armoured training Section of a Country held Ambulance by Major UM. CAZALY I.M.S. [illegible] Mr Marina Mr [illegible] on [illegible]	

Army Form C. 2118.

WAR DIARY
or
INTELLIGENCE SUMMARY

(Erase heading not required.)

Instructions regarding War Diaries and Intelligence Summaries are contained in F. S. Regs., Part II. and the Staff Manual respectively. Title Pages will be prepared in manuscript.

Place	Date	Hour	Summary of Events and Information	Remarks and references to Appendices
DAERNE	Jan 5"		Visited Royal Canadian Dragoons. 10/R.D Australian Eng B [illegible] & 9 I.T. Hussars Horse	
"	Jan 6"		Attack Any hops arrived to proceed in moving Remount P.B. men (so) as present. Home moved attention & Animon Shewed D Ank. Col. Fleming position 5th D Shewed.	
"	Jan 8"		10/RD Smith to see but Batt came to BUSVINCOURT L- inspect position Discusses where is the move there to FL Bts Showed new remit him examines	
"	Jan 11"		Position Showers shewed - G.O.C. Australian Div about Z. Arthurs L.iE country Animon where L invitations of N + X. Portland, R.H.A Arthurs	
"	Jan 12"			
"	Jan 15"		Portrails Sports/Au Shown L.A.O.C Camoon Pon cos ordered Zen Who shortly by an units	
"	Jan 16"		him A A pros L- Milton Lee G.D C.R.A hi division proposition representate Austrian lines - interview Zen Div Ambulance	

2449 Wt. W14957/M90 750,000 1/16 J.B.C. & A. Forms/C.2118/12.

WAR DIARY

Army Form C. 2118

Place	Date	Hour	Summary of Events and Information	Remarks and references to Appendices
DARNIES	Jan 17		To M&R 4/5 Division to observe fighting of field Ambulances with special reference to Amendments learned re Pan-XVIII W.E. Another received of amendment to Panjt 2 WE 2 SO German Prisoners of War at 4/25 NGRE MIER from whom medical orderly orderlies for Spain is responsible.	
	Jan 18th		Representatives reporting amendments necessary in W.E. 2 I.C. F.A. entrusted to Frenc M&R with No 3 Amendment	
	Jan 19th		To visit OC No 2 Canadian General Hospital re report	
	Jan 20th		Proceeded to GHQ	
	Jan 21st		Submitted confidentially report to Lt C.V.A MENON M.L. BHARAT Rgt (T.C.) who has returned after leave had been seen to neither by him after	
	Jan 24th		Visited M.T. Second Kennan Prisoner of War Camp which remains to is in interesting point construction by hundreds Representation up the German.	

WAR DIARY
or
INTELLIGENCE SUMMARY
(Erase heading not required.)

Place	Date	Hour	Summary of Events and Information	Remarks and references to Appendices
DARGNIES	Jan 24"		Necessary visits to South 172 & part in permutation of French Division	
"	Jan 26"		Started keeping in touch General Puijol took Sergeant Provided with Asstnt & O/C MHow & Sec. hand G.F.M. to L.H.Q. to hear lecture on herbal termes by Surgeon Macpherson	
	Jan 27"		Visited German Prisoners at war Camp with Division officer French burial & plan mcs. a French General Man is in charge. Prisoners of war Camps. It is agreed cooking ration to hours Camps in Cochenard (L.M.) were to be taken to remedy an important remark to a notice	
	Jan 30"		The weather for the past 70 days has been so bitterly severe Visited Anne Hosps & Williams Park Z. to treatment Sunday B.H. W. MONTIÈRES FARM.	

WAR DIARY or INTELLIGENCE SUMMARY

Army Form C. 2118.

Place	Date	Hour	Summary of Events and Information	Remarks and references to Appendices
DAIRGNIES	Jan 31		Proceeded to visit Australian Pioneer Battn HQ - ARMIES HQ - DUISANS 5 mile W. of ARRAS. Reconnoitred areas between [illegible] the damage (i.e. 9.30 & 4.30 approx) from [illegible] [illegible] two [illegible] offices were deputed to [illegible] [illegible] [illegible] engaged by Australian Battn. [illegible] [illegible] [illegible] [illegible] from 6 Field Armies C.R.E. [illegible] [illegible] division where returned. The General desired to [illegible] Divisional [illegible] Sapper company [illegible] to [illegible] [illegible] in [illegible] conspicuously to numerous & [illegible] [illegible] attended. Reconn Scheme but attend 67 Cavalry Division	

A.D.M.S. 5th Cavalry Division

COMMITTEE FOR THE
MEDICAL HISTORY OF THE WAR
Date 21 MAY 1917

Volume XXIII

Army Form C. 2118.

WAR DIARY
or
INTELLIGENCE SUMMARY
(Erase heading not required.)

1st Feb 1917 to 28th Feb 1917

A.D.M.S.
51st (Highland) Division

Place	Date	Hour	Summary of Events and Information	Remarks and references to Appendices
DARANIES	Feb 1		Promoted L/c M.R. & A Cavalry divisions to Acting Majors in the meantime pending ADMS	
	Feb 2		Photograph Tank Group inspected the northern frontier stores by M.H.C. A.H. Reeman, R.C. Sgt. Int. 25/1 and many more methods and numbers & reply was [illegible] the Canal and Western & E551 warehouses	
	Feb 3rd		Promoted L/c M.R. & A Cavalry divisions to see ADMS but horses L/NH Cavalry Corps	
	Feb 5-6		[illegible] Ross Road on (Africa) R. Attend L. reports on returns Causalty & a round inspections did J.N. CRUICKSHANK Roads in Sept-25 2/16 Proceeding presents in Egypt on AE as a Lt. Attend Corps Gp. hostile [illegible] Ross on F.B. men stated to Rec Divisional hee	
	Feb 6"		[illegible] Ross + [illegible] arrangements 2 Canadian OH of Patrol + Ammn Column with which there in charge	

Army Form C. 2118.

Instructions regarding War Diaries and Intelligence Summaries are contained in F. S. Regs., Part II and the Staff Manual respectively. Title Pages will be prepared in manuscript.

WAR DIARY or INTELLIGENCE SUMMARY

(Erase heading not required.)

Place	Date	Hour	Summary of Events and Information	Remarks and references to Appendices
DARGNIES	Feb 8th		D.D.M.S. Cavalry Corps visited the Divisional + inspected divnl Hospl, at BOUVAINCOURT and TULLY. Sir Ind. Purser Ruffin dep - for AUTHIEULE relieving Canadian Purser Rolston. N.W.B. Algh in medical charge.	
	Feb 10th		Promoted 6.2.N.2 1st Asst 4.S. Cavalry division. his Services position to reorganizing + amendment - necessary L. Purser Dr., Inter Establishments his sort divisional officer to Mission. Reported to Inspector gnl Mission. Reported for instruction by Mission on subject.	
	Feb 12.		Asst. C.V.A. MENON h.m.s (T.C) reports entered + reports to hr hranspar on investigations. Matter referred to him for report on amendment of Mission for consideration.	
	Feb 13th		Major - M.L. BHARAT h.m.s (G.C) reported for instruction Indian field Hospl. Purser - Ruffin thrown under Stand. G. MNON Cavalry Reld Ambulance.	
	Feb 16th		Promoted L. Cavalry Corps. Htd L. Horsman postmen to a minor hospl.	

Army Form C. 2118.

WAR DIARY
or
INTELLIGENCE SUMMARY

(Erase heading not required.)

Instructions regarding War Diaries and Intelligence Summaries are contained in F.S. Regs., Part II. and the Staff Manual respectively. Title Pages will be prepared in manuscript.

Place	Date	Hour	Summary of Events and Information	Remarks and references to Appendices
DARGNIES	Feb 17"		The Divisional General Visited our Cavalry Regt & Ambulances of the Division & observed his satisfaction with Their appearance in turn out.	
	Feb 19"		Proceeded into District & an Officers Mess, G.H.Q. & a meeting of Various Officers of Cavalry Division by invitation of Lt Col Robertson. Lt Col Kerr & Major next to Major L. Cavalry L.I.K. CRADY H.M.S & the necessity for reorganization of Cavalry Field Ambulance.	
	Feb 19"		Attack Cavalry Corps arrived & received Fresh Remounts. Section of Mobile Cavalry Det of Ambulance.	
	Feb 21"		Capt H.M.S Rennay Paul started & 14 Jany instruction into horse operation put a pieces of Mathers & its annual his pain & Distant which & Distant as a Veterinary	
	Feb 25"		Visited 7" A.V. & 8am Officers Cmdg reported to remember to heregt again - Criteria.	

2449 Wt. W14957/Mg0 750,000 1/16 J.B.C. & A. Forms/C.2118/12.

WAR DIARY
INTELLIGENCE SUMMARY

Army Form C. 2118.

Place	Date	Hour	Summary of Events and Information	Remarks and references to Appendices
Avesnes	20/2/16		Inspected Posts manned by Sentry Committee held conference proposed to interview O.C.S. to see an improved & practical operation further designed by Capt Smalley sent to members to points to trench in Sheaffram. This Table to be members to attempts to din am. the Frontalalong positions is permitted, & no in the respects important to the potations issued want to be field machine site, and to see Fable to attempts be supplied to hostiemen has Staram for Fire —	
			Met the 7 Devon 4th Canady Army with representatives to 2 French division from Wyck & Corps HQ at FC Prescinine LeerCamp at YZENGREMER where, to remember to attempts report to him were made on existing sanitary conditions, which are in an entire[?] satisfactory state.	
"	21/2/16		Proceeded was a junction 4" Cavalry divn to Authiewle Halloy & ARNEZ-LES-DUISANS to inspect Platoon Billets & the field entrenchments & camped Thaies[?].	

WAR DIARY or INTELLIGENCE SUMMARY

Army Form C. 2118.

Place	Date	Hour	Summary of Events and Information	Remarks and references to Appendices
Barfleur	20/5/28		The following T.C. Officer Ranks arrived to complete establishment + were posted as under.	
			Capt. J. G. MACDONALD-FIRTH Ranked (T.C.) to MHOW. C.F.A	
			Capt. J. MAGNER Ranked (T.C.) to SEC'BAD C.F.A	
				Symonds Bn Col. Int. Adjutant 8th Cavalry Division

*COMMITTEE FOR THE
MEDICAL HISTORY OF THE WAR
Date -6 JUL. 1917*

Army Form C. 2118.

Volume XXVIII

A.D.M.S. 5th Cav Division

WAR DIARY
or
INTELLIGENCE SUMMARY

(Erase heading not required.)

1st to 31st March 1917

Place	Date	Hour	Summary of Events and Information	Remarks and references to Appendices
DARANTES	Mar 1		Sec'd al C.F.A relieves MNSW C.F.A in Ariel trench at Bouvancourt.	
"	Mar 2		D.D.M.S Cavalry Corps inspects Canadian Para mounted Sections Administration Staff Osserin Led at Mont Neuf Quartier.	
"	Mar 4		Recommendations for Honours Rewards for period Sep 25. 1917 submitted to 3 rd M.Gr. Separate return sent for period Sept 21. 1916 to correspond with those submitted by Sec'tal C.F.A during absence work up of Sec'tal at Shorncliffe. Between Nov 10. 1916. Acting in connection the movement of motor Ambulances Brentine hos-day of the to U. in employment Puntar Park for Shell Shock.	
"	Mar 5		Held monthly meet Room on P.B. Intn.	
"	Mar 6		Capt HMS Ramay Ramer DADMS returns to train formation he has been attacked from HRD DX Ambulance from 14 Meap	

2449 Wt. W14957/M90 750,000 1/16 J.B.C. & A. Forms/C.2118/12.

Army Form C. 2118.

WAR DIARY
or
INTELLIGENCE SUMMARY
(Erase heading not required.)

Place	Date	Hour	Summary of Events and Information	Remarks and references to Appendices
DALHONIES	Mar 7th		Presentation of ribbons to those awarded decorations was made by Brigadiers in the afternoon the M.G.C. men from the F.As attended the parades of their respective Brigades.	Appx 1
	Mar 8		Col. A.T. MacNeil. (N.S. left for leave, called by D.D.M.S. office Cav. Corps to see a new pattern stretcher. Lieut-Col A.N. Fleming (M.S. officials a/A.D.M.S.	Appx 1
		9.30	D.A.D.M.S. in company with the O.C. No.15 Ambulance Wren Camp inspected the sanitary condition of the camp and marked improvement.	Appx 1
		3 Pt	A.D.M.S. & D.A.D.M.S. attended a conference at D.D.M.S. Cav. Corps — the question of what kind of stretcher to be carried by mounted units was discussed — it was decided that the division should carry remain as at present but that other divisions should carry an improvised stretcher composed of two French stretchers & that the P.M.S. should carry 8 in addition to 6 lance stretchers (so carried in the 2 haversacks) which we much to prepare to account of 8 horse which	Appx 1
	13	3.30	D.A.D.M.S. inspected billets of the 1st Cair Horse & found every thing satisfactory.	Appx 1

Army Form C. 2118.

WAR DIARY
or
INTELLIGENCE SUMMARY
(Erase heading not required.)

Instructions regarding War Diaries and Intelligence Summaries are contained in F. S. Regs., Part II. and the Staff Manual respectively. Title Pages will be prepared in manuscript.

Place	Date	Hour	Summary of Events and Information	Remarks and references to Appendices
DARGNIES	March 15th		D.A.D.M.S. made a sanitary inspection of the billets of the 9th DRAGOONS at MAISNIERES & found everything satisfactory.	W.I.S.A.
	16		D.A.D.M.S. made a sanitary inspection of billets at E.F.A & 15th reserved LONGROY & made some recommendations to the M.O.	W.I.S.A.
	—	19	Orders for the Canadian Bde with C.F.A & more than received at 7.30 a.m. The Canadian Divis in all move forward to	W.I.S.A.
		20	The I.F.A. moved today. Its area being approx SE NARPONT the Canadian C.F.A. being with its Brigade in the NESLE No 2 Divisional Head Quarters arrived at DARGNIES MANDEUSBAIRE. Divisional H.Q. moved to PONTDEMETZ being at 1 C.F.A & REBILLED with 1 C.F.A.	W.I.S.A.
		21		
		22	Orders received at 6 p.m. & the I.C.F.A. & more from at 10.30 MHOW C.F.A. & Sanitary Sectn to CACHY. Sec'd at C.F.A. to GENTELLES. the A.D.M.S office moved CERISY. A.D.M.S visited D.M.Str & Arrangements made for Canadian C.F.A. were under to that Mhow C.F.A. & Canadian Bridges.	
		23	Orders received that the normal or return from leave Col. A. Macnab reported H.Q. this morning an orders of G.O.C then respective Bridges. an A.D.M.S. of the Division	

2449 Wt. W14957/M90 750,000 1/16 J.B.C. & A. Forms/C.2118/12.

WAR DIARY
INTELLIGENCE SUMMARY

Army Form C. 2118.

Place	Date	Hour	Summary of Events and Information	Remarks and references to Appendices
Peronne	23rd		The Division moved forward through to positions:	
			Arthur Canadian Bde — NALLE	
			Trumpets Bde — B. de MEREAUCOURT	
			See. Ho? B.R. — GENTELLES	
			Divnl M.G. — PERONNE	
			Fld Ambulance — with — Tam respective Bdes	
			Saw. Section — HERBECOURT	
"	24th		Arthur's Bde move onMOISLAINS	
			ESTREES-EN-CHAUSSEES. M Now O.F.A. Stored at MONS-EN	
			CHAUSSEE.	
			Canadian Bde HQ at MOISLAINS Canadian C.F.A	
			stored in a brick-kiln ½ mile S. E. MOISLAINS	
			Yesterday HQ- Anzac moved Arthur III & IV Corps	
			No. 36 C.C.S. at CAYEUX & MAIN Steam Rd at PROYART	
			Arthur's MNow O.F.A. Proceeded L. N/R 32nd Division at	
			NESLE & surrounds. Preliminary arrangements for evacuation	
			& Canadians complete. Am nearly arrive in respect to	
			evacuation. Exffords NESLE — CAYEUX — main routes	

WAR DIARY
or
INTELLIGENCE SUMMARY

Army Form C. 2118.

Place	Date	Hour	Summary of Events and Information	Remarks and references to Appendices
PÉRONNE	25th	—	Proceeded L. Army Head Quarters to arrange one route of Observation for Riflemen & other Ranks to be detailed for Observation, then obtaining the division of A section hammocks ink-subsection at CAYEUX & BRAY as proper originals, and economising medical personnel, for direct evacuation to BRAY or Reserve as from Canadian & Sec Genl C.F.A are concerned, whilst MHOW C.F.A uses the Southmidlothian F.A. in PÉRONNE as a Relay Posn. for Walking on route to BRAY, & houses British evacuation if necessary through the route.	
"	26th		Visited Sec. Genl C.F.A whose war hospital address the hunt, rate occasion to the Commanding Officer. Saw M.Zipinks Lemon Marthe L-4 Duty. Between for an act of devotion to duty made from W of GINCHY CORNER on Aug 11th 1916. MNTH C.F.A on Aulnoy Ammunition m. MUNS.EN. CHAUSSE Canadian	
"	27th		M- MUSLAINS with Rifle occupied EQUANCOURT & ETRICOURT. Canadian Cav war evacuated L. BRAY down. YTRES on 26th with personnel their GUEYENCOURT and SAULCOURT on 25th. Canadians moved LIERAMONT into FAUCON of other Duty for 8th Hussars and this Ambulance Rifle into VILLERS- further evacuated with L.A.C. Buffets were employed, into not heavy was he Matter.	

Army Form C. 2118.

WAR DIARY
or
INTELLIGENCE SUMMARY
(Erase heading not required.)

Place	Date	Hour	Summary of Events and Information	Remarks and references to Appendices
PERONNE	27		Motion arrangements were as follows:- MNOW C.F.A opened an A.D.S. dressing station in - W. end of TINCOURT. "A" Tent-Section remained at - MONS-EN-CHAUSSÉE - Regtl Aid Posts - R.O.P. however on walking wounded of VILLERS-FAUCON - By agreement - with - "48th Divn British ambulance evacuated L. Sections walking from PERONNE. Return to C.C.S. at BRAY via S/M F.A. at PERONNE. At A Relay Post. Procured water after A/C G.O. to find Capt J. RONAN of L.A.C. Ruling reported wounded at A.D.S. determined his immediate evacuation to Peronne. Met - motor ambulance cars, or via his officer & 3 men of his unit. (- and later removed to Watermere his signal wounded.) Returned MONS-EN-CHAUSSÉE via PERONNE. Several Capt-Ronans ministries informed & now A.D.C.C.S at BRAY; for that evening abdominal injuries had become too great to wait. From the Southern F.A. Arrived at A.D.S. at 1.30 am.	
"	28		SEC'BAD Pull with "A" C.F.A. in reserve moved to - hourwise between CLERY & FRISE from MNOW C.F.A in bivouac between they dressing stations for the wet - in TINCOURT- air bus- lynx- casualties from - PERONNE, and for Tent-section at MONS-EN-CHAUSSÉE. Walking to bussable lightly wounded at - Visite Ambulance Rall M.O. met for	
"	29		Procured" No 43 C.C.S. BRAY 2- overtime conditions J. RONAN with a Pneumonia. A short account previous walking	

2449 Wt. W14957/M90 750,000 1/16 J.B.C. & A. Forms/C.2118/12.

WAR DIARY / INTELLIGENCE SUMMARY

Army Form C. 2118

Place	Date	Hour	Summary of Events and Information	Remarks and references to Appendices
PERONNE	29th		After penetrating 3/8 inch armour. Matrix had entered expecting report /with below aeroplane containing sent this and missing his someone in sunlight in the limbs on - 4 mists by aeroplane enter and by army. Sixteen in mentioned to improve. Serves has been attacked on PERONNE. An inspection from them in establishment search, or of persevarants on moonset. Serves had been with teammates from - mentioned. Mislays his programmes is free. Total Casualties of the ranks (Battle Casualties only) Noon 25th to Noon 28th: Officers (a) British (b) Indian (a) Killed – Wounded – Missing (b) 1 – 7 – 1 Other Ranks (a) Br. (b) Indian Killed – Wounded – Missing (a) 8 4 – (b) 2 6 – Noon 26th – Noon 27th: Officers (a) Br. (b) Indian Killed – Wounded – Missing (a) – 2 – (b) – 1 – Other Ranks (a) Br. (b) Indian Killed – Wounded – Missing (a) 4 9 – (b) – 7 1 Noon 27th – Noon 28th: Officers (a) Br. (b) Indian Killed – Wounded – Missing (a) – 4 – (b) – – – Other Ranks (a) Br. (b) Indian Killed – Wounded – Missing (a) 3 41 – (b) 1 1 – Ambulance Cars, Btn. transport, bivouacs Casualties " " BOIS DE MARÉCAU COURT were CAPPY	K.W.M Br.Officers – 6 – Ind. " – 1 – Br.O.R. 4 63 7 Ind. O.R. 1 1 07 Total All Ranks Killed Wounded Missing 5 75 140

WAR DIARY
or
INTELLIGENCE SUMMARY.

Place	Date	Hour	Summary of Events and Information	Remarks and references to Appendices
VILLERS-BRETONNEUX	30th		The Division moved headquarters this morning - MARCEL EN VILLERS BRETONNEUX; Ambulance Pits into MNOW C.F.A in WARFUSÉE - ABANCOURT Sec: hospital into 1st C.F.A in BAYONVILLERS, Evacuation in CAPPY. Stay Section in CAPPY. Guiberman is third 149&5 in 4 km.	
"	31.0.		Another under the latest war establishment. Kept orders to Reg. 6- and dismounted in rest - with Reg to make necessary arrangements for him. The Motor Ammunition Section of the MNOW C.F.A when moving from MONS-EN-CHAUSSÉE to TINCOURT should have proceeded as convoluted under instructions received from this office. After leaving at short resumes of the movement of the motor terrain division the personnel this happens learned, and was placed as that the evidence it to have been very unto rather.	

(signed) Edmunds
Brevet Colonel
A/just 5th Cav Bde
1.R.S.

COMMITTEE FOR THE
MEDICAL HISTORY OF THE WAR
Date - 6 JUL. 1917

Volume XXIX / Vol 29

Army Form C. 2118.

WAR DIARY
INTELLIGENCE SUMMARY.
(Erase heading not required.)

A.D.M.S. 5th (Cdn) Division

Place	Date	Hour	Summary of Events and Information	Remarks and references to Appendices
VILLERS-BRETONNEUX	April 1st		Visited 8th Hussars + M&SH C.F.A. Sanitary section arrived at VILLERS BRETONNEUX	
"		3rd	Major D.P. KAPELLE O/C Canadian C.F.A. proceeded on 10 days leave on urgent private affair	
"		4th	D.A.D.M.S. visited Canadian Field Amb. + divisional C.C.S. at BRAY. Reinforcements rejoined the division from GAMACHES	
"		7th	Proceeded to 4th Army H.Q. to see A.M.S	
"		11th	Visited 18th Lancers, M.&SH C.F.A, Sec'd & C.F.A + Rifle M&D and divisional C.C.S. The division received orders to move forward to ?	
"		12th	Orders put move cancelled owing to Ref weather	
"		13th	Visited Amb. 4th Army preparing to move battalions to to divn have not been relieved	
			The division moved to an area of concentration this morning	
GUIZANCOURT		16th	Visited M&D and no 1 at GUIZANCOURT. Field Ambulances are with their respective Brigades in general. Sec'd C.F.A. 1/2 mile N.W. of GUIZANCOURT. Canadian C.F.A. at ATHIES	
			TREFCON M&SH C.F.A. at CAULANCOURT, Canadian C.F.A. at ATHIES Sanitary Section is with divn M&D	

WAR DIARY

INTELLIGENCE SUMMARY

Place	Date	Hour	Summary of Events and Information	Remarks and references to Appendices
QUIRANCOURT	15th April		Visited an C.F.A & Fd Divisions, admin 5D" divisn, & OC 2nd/3rd North midld F.A. at STEREN. Discuss arrangements for the provision from an forward MHow C.F.A. is speed for sick of ambulce at See (w) Regts, Canadian C.F.A. for sick of Canadian OR. See'hd C.F.A in Liaison with now evacuates to Senstismeters F.A. at PERONNE and & Rely Post, Steffalmete & sick are evacuated by motor Ambulance Convoy. British Sick are evacuated b- 2/1st North midland F.A. at STEREN, stufr-cases travel by arrangement with Ambul 5D" down sent z Adv Rest Stn at VILLERS-CARBONNEL. OC Canadian C.F.A. finds 1 M.O. & 1st O.R. for M.D.S at STEREN; OC MHow C.F.A finds 1 SAS 1/ Indian nursing orderly b- as- an interpreter at Rly Post at-PERONNE	
"	16th April		Visited Advd 35th Division at BEAUVOIS. Instructions of EUSOL in treatment of wounds; in returns for the prevention of Pyorreae & Scurvy; to his own of specialigns "Fisher" for over inmates to be ensured.	
"	19th April		Visited D.D.M.S. 6" Corps	
"	20th April		Informal venture begins. Visited Sec bd C.F.A & 2" Anyram Guard	
"	21st		Special instructions for prevention of 24. troches. & on semitary measures in general circulated to all units.	

Army Form C. 2118.

WAR DIARY
INTELLIGENCE SUMMARY.
(Erase heading not required.)

Instructions regarding War Diaries and Intelligence Summaries are contained in F. S. Regs., Part II. and the Staff Manual respectively. Title pages will be prepared in manuscript.

Place	Date	Hour	Summary of Events and Information	Remarks and references to Appendices
GUZAUCOURT	Nov 23		Visited Canadian Rest, Hospital & 2nd 2 Berry Horse	
"	24		Visited Shetland Horse, Royal Canadian Dragoons, also Ambulance Rate, Minor C.F.A. & 18th Lancers	
"	26		Specific instructions issued to L. Browne Ambulances & Omnibus Convoy and a source of treatment uses	
"	28		Total sick admissions to hospital for week ending this day: B.O. 1.0 B.O.R. I.O.R. 2 - 535 13 Total No. Evacuated during the week B.O. 1.0. B.O.R. I.O.R. 2 - 21 13 Average strength of division for the week British 7626 Indian 2,921	
"	29		Visited Sec. Gen. Rifle Bde 148th xx'th Decan Horse & Sec. 6"x C.F.A.	
"	30		Visited O/C 6/15 Airli. Samy Section. Arrangements concerning from pen over of 4th Army & arranges co-operation measures with him, also for medical Stores & tire items to which in workshops & L.o' the seven ambulance motor & gleam of minim field ambulance. Veh. stands in 4 Corps, & third 4.5 Army, And to telepraime Gic Medsean	

Place	Date	Hour	Summary of Events and Information	Remarks and references to Appendices
GUIZANCOURT	30		Horse & vehicle camp lines as with the offices lines. Cavalry did Andrews Maneuver. The General visited the Division Ammunition Column which had recently Join'd the Division from its fitter Move to Horse of April. Considering the severe weather Horses have been remarkably fit. [signed] Brigadier General Adjut'd Cavalry Division	

A.D.M.S., 5th London Div.

COMMITTEE FOR THE
MEDICAL HISTORY OF THE WAR
Date 27 JUL 1917

Army Form C. 2118.

WAR DIARY
INTELLIGENCE SUMMARY
(Erase heading not required.)

Volume XXX
A.D.M.S. 5th Can'n Div'n
15 to 31st May 1917

Place	Date	Hour	Summary of Events and Information	Remarks and references to Appendices
GUERANCOURT	1st	a.m. p.m.	Visited MNOW C.F.A. with D.A.D.M.S. — made a thorough inspection of lines of Cdn. Canadian Artillerymen in company with D.A.D.M.S.; S.M.O. Canadian Corps R.H.A. & h. O. 2 Art Regt. Within this sanitary instructions were by 2nd MSV. had been inspected, things had rather been improved from time to time. and these instructions carried out to the bivouac & precautions against ONIANON tracts were emphasized, his attention to the OBrigade Commander was drawn & his attention of Lieutenant Sebregondi to O.C. his Regt. was drawn also to the necessity of such sanitation to be considered essential to the bivouac & to a proper movement of assistance to his machine gunners to the execution of his duties was made to him. Similarly yesterday morning D.A.D.M.S. made an inspection of his lines & bivouacs of his 7th Dragoon Guards & reports his sanitary arrangements interments are in a satisfactory condition. His instructions conveyed & think orders are now being strictly carried out. The previous report were perfectly noticed (a) Latrines were not fly-proof and of satisfactory type. (b) Manure was not being properly	

WAR DIARY or INTELLIGENCE SUMMARY

Army Form C. 2118.

Place	Date	Hour	Summary of Events and Information	Remarks and references to Appendices
GUIZANCOURT	May 3rd		[illegible handwritten entry] (c) As the officers in charge 'A' Evacuation the chauffeurs very sick. Arrangements for the third Lorry Section has been seen — First week and a second instruction with a lorry to make visit to other Lorry.	
"	May 4th		Visited Ambulance at HAM & CAULAINCOURT, & arranged for FODEN Lorry to proceed there from NESLE, its services being now available for Sec[ond] Cav[alry] Bde. Ordered M. TREFCON in W.R., & the Cavalry Bde Castel at ATHIES to reopen. Officer Comdg Field Ambulance & M.O. of Regt. visited office, & Workshops & O.C. 61st M. Amb. Courtesy Section & three subordinate members of personnel inspected. Gas drying appliance. Arrangements known have been made by Works Section for Field Ambulance now open. External morphia & practical Btn of public motor cars portable latrine covers, Wy frost Field ovens, sterilisers, bunkers in one Lorry, etc.	
"	May 5th		3 Coms of Sanitary Companies reported as entrusted with Septum Customs. C.C.S. the situation of an active officer has been shown to be receiving... the opinion of Workshops bears on a subaltern for Crane.	

Army Form C. 2118.

WAR DIARY
or,
INTELLIGENCE SUMMARY.
(Erase heading not required.)

Instructions regarding War Diaries and Intelligence Summaries are contained in F. S. Regs., Part II. and the Staff Manual respectively. Title pages will be prepared in manuscript.

Place	Date	Hour	Summary of Events and Information	Remarks and references to Appendices
GUIZANCOURT	May 5"		[illegible handwritten entry regarding inspections, hygiene of the month, etc.]	
"	May 6"		ADMS O/C 61st Sanitary Section L-Divide visited the area in CAUCAINCOURT. May be used for bathing, but considered not fit for use on account of permitted source L-Snd & army regulations. Arrangements made for inspection of OMIGNON River where are not being employed. Orders sent with instructions to regiment were issued by the Division inspected huts 7-78" Divison & Directed them in PELVES to that the area round the huts L- present pollution from french zone area.	
	May 8"		R.H.A & R.C.H.A Brigades with train Ammn Column proceeded L- III Corps Area and are under L- 59" Division under orders L- R.E. RA III Corps American Officer accompanied Lieut Col. Weir D.D.M.S III Corps L- report horses & area/sim medical arrangements AM Dismounted Reinforcements team have L- 7" D.G., L-	

2353 Wt. W3544/1454 700,000 5/15 D. D. & L. A.D.S.S./Forms/C. 2118.

WAR DIARY
or
INTELLIGENCE SUMMARY

(Erase heading not required.)

Army Form C. 2118.

Place	Date	Hour	Summary of Events and Information	Remarks and references to Appendices
CUZANCOURT	8th	8 a.m.	Horses moved to neighbouring Rues D'HURNON, out with [?] employed in defences. O.C. 72 M.G. Coy Section has been communicated with re further vehicle drivers & travelling.	
	9th		Visit today of 34th Punjab Horse.	
		10.	Orders issued for the formation of two Armoured Brigades from two Divns. which with three units seemed to be on forever. Being held by SD "L" 35th Division. Cavalry Corps via forward reps — III Corps, & the Armrd Cars of Cavalry will be amended in K.B. & reinforcements were L.K. North of H. [?] Affds SD: Division would advance drawing 8th in — BERNES ROUGE	
	11th		and JEANCOURT. Learnt mention of Regtl ad Posts, & times to see Arms. Proceeded to — III Corps M.I. to see Arms [?]	
		12th	Had several Cavalry Corps on III Corps M.I. , went round with own later with two Latts of given hot advice 32nd Division with VERMAND advance therewith in — VADENCOURT, with him, & arranged to [?] together [?] advance on 14th. Troops were within camouflage [?] for ward to Wing of Cavalry Div Ambulances.	

WAR DIARY
INTELLIGENCE SUMMARY

Place	Date	Hour	Summary of Events and Information	Remarks and references to Appendices
GUIZANCOURT	May 13		Copies of hectic arrangements for 57th minute Brigade and Ambulances relieving C.F.A. antedates 2-am internal. Spent morning with Asst. Director Cavalry Corps & visited BOUVINCOURT, ROISEL, ST CREN, VILLERS-CARBONNEL, and Trek & Kitting 4" Cavalry Divn Leaves Arny H.Q. 2- divisions ambulances to leave on operation received.	
	May 14		Asst ADMS 4 Cav Div arrived, & agreed L- plans over to his C.F.A. in STCREN new him themin - SR to brk Cavly turning to for 51st Div in the West. ADMS Asst themin - Zei J Cavln C.F.A took over VADENCOURT from 35th divn. Tent section J town ambulance reinforcements on MERAUCOURT.	
NOBESCOURT FARM	May 15		Asst ADMS moved here this day. See'd 4 C.F.A Asst themin for LoK over JEANCOURT anum. Jn section over near STCREN from 51st Division. Capt WHS Binney Ravine dept returns from leave, Visits w-- Asths STCREN Avt arranged with ADMS 51st divn from 2 M.O. + 36 O.R L- new Divns O.C. for 2nd C.F.A. leave here	

Army Form C. 2118.

WAR DIARY
or
INTELLIGENCE SUMMARY.

Place	Date	Hour	Summary of Events and Information	Remarks and references to Appendices
NURESCOURT FARM	May 16		Dist: III Corps in ÉTOREN. Also visited M&M CFA in LAU LAINCOURT within command. From Advd H.Q. went for by INDEN COURT and the command; VADENCOURT, & Regtl Aid Posts in Quarry; approved Canadian R.E. Wks; thence to renew SgR ad JEANCOURT and Sec'd but R.A.C. HQ & and permit train scheme of medical arrangements has been undertaken by Bde Bde and in conjunction with B.M. conferring in connection with HQ &n to R.C.A. were in occupation of to accommodations needed for Regtl Aid Post in during APRIL M.S.A. Came to an agreement regarding the HQ - O.C. and Bde M&n. A Regtl Regtl Aid Post for the 2nd Bde (approx'd by had have) commenced necessary and arrange location of and with R.E.	
"	May 17		Brigadiers forwarded to see Aid Posts (first) and the mentioned sanitary orders with reports to the forwards, and accommodation in particular	
"	May 18		using to property of Regts & Companies H&R. Matron Gen Cotton arrived and proceeded to visit his units in company who detailed him there to Op Stary Section	

WAR DIARY or INTELLIGENCE SUMMARY

Place	Date	Hour	Summary of Events and Information	Remarks and references to Appendices
MORBECOURT FARM	May 19		The Division went under the Administration of Cavalry Corps (from 10/5/17). Hrs: Attack 4/1 Cavalry Division between co-operation ? hrs IX (9). Posn - at 4.20 & 4.33 with attacks & O.C. attached trench Ran at VRANCOURT.	
"	May 20		Visited attack Cavalry Corps with attack 4/1 Cavalry Division and prepared a line of positions approaching which at one to approaches to heavy bombardment [illegible], which in his view even the 4 Anti-Roy Station, & a bombardment [illegible] common & at 4.5 & 5.5 Divisions. Re-position assured that persuasion by attack Corps to recommence fire with attack 4/5 Army.	
"	May 21		Inspected Canadian C.F.A. at MEREAUCOURT then accommodation for 30 cars & [illegible]. Visited MIKON C.F.A. & 13/15 Gunners.	
"	May 22		Visited Canadian Anti-Aircraft Armory Section at VADENCOURT and Regt'l All Posts & Quarry. Arranged for supply of some [illegible] R.E. stores to Anti-A.C., & for further ammunition/[illegible] storage at PONTRU Supply Refilling & to Brotheneau B.K. N/D.	

WAR DIARY
INTELLIGENCE SUMMARY

Army Form C. 2118.

Place	Date	Hour	Summary of Events and Information	Remarks and references to Appendices
MONESCOURT FARM	Aug 23		Visited with 14th H[us]s[ars] Cavalry Corps Patrol traversing point at VENDICOURT and VADANCOURT — MOISLAINS — MT CANISNICOURT — Communication MT ST GERMAIN. Records contained in yesterday's main itinerary from 4th + 5th Dragoons in vicinity of BERNES. Received report from General that 11th + 15th Dragoons with [illegible] to attack in conjunction with 23rd Inf[antry] Regt are attacking and encountered enemy infantry and MG on outskirts of ESSIGNY-LE-GRAND... in the vicinity of VENDICOURT... no further news, but from the Regt 372nd Inf[antry] Div[ision]... action, Main itinerary [illegible] reported... Brigade was found to attack with... found to die without news in regard to SUNRERIS road as N.W. of BERNES attempt [illegible] from Corps Group. Staff as then reported... infantry and heavy... reported to attack later.	

Place	Date	Hour	Summary of Events and Information	Remarks and references to Appendices
MORISSCOURT FARM	May 25		Prepared Sanitary Report for the fortnight. Visited hygienic en-chef 57th Divn French Army which is on our right & arranged combined action regarding measures necessary for the protection of to unknown River. The French ready to help leave our men debts on the Right bank.	
"	May 26		Visited the Sucrerie BERNES with A.D.M.S. S.C. Sec'n Lieut C.F.A. also to ascertain & have thorough Sanitation. Visited site of new main dressing Sta. there then site of Huts. Supply Stores also 34 C.C.S. & 36 Mort Ambulance Survey at TINCOURT, GPs Scottish Sta. & Respiration Pat 2nd & 3rd Cavalry divisions at DOINGT & huntmans C.C.S at LA CHAPELETTE.	
"	May 27		A successful assignment on river sent to Hd 2rd Bn no dirt there, two nights with SWKs Bn (1 time) + 4 minutes bny of Minz returned 6 July. 11 hermann were killed by rifle fire & no bayonet & others — number not known — by our artillery fire; 7 prisoners were taken. Visited Canadian Front during afternoon with O.C. 2nd Staffordshire there	

Place	Date	Hour	Summary of Events and Information	Remarks and references to Appendices
NOBESCOURT FARM	May 27		& found that medical arrangements had been carried out, assisted were promptly rendered, & wounded speedily evacuated. An Advanced Regtl Aid Post had been established N-TWIN CRATERS R.6.a.6.1 after there 6- which wounded were carried by hand. A 2nd Aid Post in Quarry R.11.a.3.4 could be reached by wheeled stretcher bearers, and by a relay of bearers to the Advanced Dressing Stn VADENCOURT R.16.a.9.4. All wounded received other treatment one hour. After examining Stn, Quarry & Twin Craters, Also Tumulus Punter Wood & sprinkler area. Incoming casualties were reported to R.I. 34th Norse Rind 3 wounded 4 9th Horse wounded 5	
"	May 28		Arranged for a party from Sang Section to Nonebet to assist for work in huts in SWERERIE BERNES on being requested by Infantry. O.C. SECOND C.F.A. the force over invented O.C. Sang Section as & inverse of reinforcement required.	
"	May 29		Visited Advanced R.A.P. A/P.R. & Advanced C.F.A.	

Army Form C. 2118.

WAR DIARY
or
INTELLIGENCE SUMMARY.
(Erase heading not required.)

Instructions regarding War Diaries and Intelligence Summaries are contained in F. S. Regs., Part II. and the Staff Manual respectively. Title pages will be prepared in manuscript.

Place	Date	Hour	Summary of Events and Information	Remarks and references to Appendices
NOREUIL FARM	May 30		Battalion rested with no material change + remained in support to 27. STEREN [?]	
	May 31		Battalion rested. The Brigade was in Divisional Reserve + on exercise right to 4.5 Buckshire had necessary adjustment in personnel. Refit drawn. Lectures 6 + 9 officers to ATBush from Major C. F. N. on June 1st. Promotion taken up by Arthur + "C" Coy 2nd Lieutenants Athol... C. Cushman... A. Cushman as Captains to Australian training School; Athol... Seconded to the Promotion casualties in action since previous June [?] from [?] to Sept the month.
Officers:
OR Ranks Indian
British - Indian K.W.M. Indian
K.W.M. K.W.M. 8.22.1
7.45 ...
- 4. - -2 -	

Commanding [signature]
27th Division

No.2232/17.

Copy No..........

G.O.C. Sec'bad Cavalry Brigade.
  "   Canadian   "   "
  "   Ambala   "   "

SECRET

Reference Map1/40,000, Sheet 62.c.

With reference to 5th Cavalry Divisions Nos.G.S.570/4 and G&S.573/1 dated May 10th and 11th respectively the following Medical personnel, transport, and equipment is at your disposal. Will you please issue the necessary instructions to all concerned except to Cav'y Field Ambulances and Sanitary Section which are receiving orders direct:-

SEC'BAD CAVALRY BRIGADE.

Medical Officers.............. Capt.J.J.Magner.R.A.M.C., 7th Dragoon Gds, Senior Medical Officer,
Lieut.W.A.Reardon.I.M.S. 18th Lancers.
Lieut.S.A.Phatak.I.M.S. 34th Poona Horse.

Sub-Asst-Surgeons........... { from 20th Deccan Horse.
                              { from 9th Hodson's Horse.

Ward Orderlies.............. { from 34th Poona Horse.
                              { from 18th Lancers.

British Orderlies for Medical Officers:- 2 from 7th Dragoon Guards.

Stretcher Bearers:-32 (8 from 7th Dragoon Gds, 6 per Indian Regt.)

For Sanitary duties:- 2.B.O.R.from 7th Dragoon Guards, 6 Indians from Div'l Sanitary Section.

R.A.M.C., for water duties:-2.B.O.R.from 7th Dragoon Gds.

Batmen for Medical Officers....3.

TRANSPORT

Two half G.S.Limbered wagons for Medical Equipment.

Two water carts complete..... { 1 from Sec'bad I.C.F.A.
                               { 1 "   Mhow   "

EQUIPMENT

Three sets of the following to be supplied by the M.B. 18th Lancers 34th Poona Horse and Sec'bad I.C.F.A.:-

3 Pairs Field Medical Panniers.... 1 pair from Sec'bad I.C.F.A.
                                   1 "   "   M.O. 18th Lancers.
                                   1 "   "   M.O. 34th Poona Horse.

3 Field Service Haversacks......... -------- do --------
3   "   Medical Companions........ -------- do --------
3 Haversacks, Shell Dressings...... -------- do --------
18 Field Stretchers................ from Sec'bad I.C.F.A.
100 Ammonia Capsules............... ------- do --------

P.T.O.

CANADIAN CAVALRY BRIGADE.

Medical Officers.......... { Capt. W.J.E. Mingie. C.A.M.C.
{ Capt. E.C. Whitehouse. C.A.M.C.

Orderlies for duty with M.O's.... 2 from R.C. Dragoons.
                                            2 " F.G. Horse.

C.A.M.C., for water duties...... 2 from L.S. Horse.

Stretcher Bearers............... 20.:-
                                         8 from L.S. Horse.
                                         6 " R.C. Dragoons.
                                         6 " F.G. Horse.

Sanitary Orderlies.............. 2 per Regiment.

TRANSPORT.

Two half G.S. Limbered Wagons for Medical Equipment.

Two water-carts complete..... { 1 from Canadian.C.F.A.
{ 1 " Canadian Brigade.

EQUIPMENT.

~~2~~ pairs Field Medical Panniers.... 1 ~~pair from Canadian C.F.A.~~
                                      1 " " M.O. R.C. Dragoons.
                                      1 " " M.O. F.G. Horse.
2 ~~3~~ Field ~~Service~~ *Surgical* Haversacks....... - - - - - -do- - - - - -
2 ~~3~~ Field Medical Companions...... - - - - - -do- - - - - -
2 ~~3~~ Haversacks, Shell Dressings.... - - - - - -do- - - - - -
12 Field Stretchers.............. from Canadian.C.F.A.
50 Ammonia Capsules.............. - - - -do- - - -

2. Movements and dispositions of Field Ambulances which are now Divisional Units, will be as follows:-

__SEC'BAD.I.C.F.A.__
           The Advanced Dressing Station of this Unit will take over the Advanced Dressing Station at JEANCOURT from 59th Division on 15th inst. Advanced party to arrive at noon. The Tent Section will report to A.D.M.S., 59th Division at BOUVINCOURT the same day, and will work in conjunction with the Infantry Field Ambulance there established. Wheeled Stretcher Carriers will be taken with the Advanced Dressing Station. Indian casualties will also be admitted, light cases and casual sick being transferred to Mhow I.B.F.A.

Regimental Aid Posts in this Sector are as under:-
   (a) In sunken road.W. of Wood in L.28.a.Central.
   (b) At L.33.d.0.3.
   Hand carriage of casualties from Regimental Aid Post to Advanced Dressing Station, thence by Motor Ambulances to BOUVINCOURT.

__CANADIAN.C.F.A.__
           The Advanced Dressing Station of this Unit will take over the Advanced Dressing Station at VADENCOURT (R.16.a.9.4. on the 14th inst. Advanced party to arrive at noon that day, remainder moving in the same evening at dusk. All wheeled trans less 1 Motor Ambulance to return to VERMAND. Officer commanding Mhow I.C.F.A. will place 4 Wheeled Stretcher Carriers at disposal of O.C. Canadian C.F.A., for use with the Advanced Dressing Station Regimental Aid Posts at R.11.a.8.4. Hand carriage of casualties by wheeled stretcher carriers to advanced dressing station.

                                                                               P.T.O.

Thence by motor ambulance to Mhow I.C.F.A. at CAULAINCOURT. O.C. Advanced Dressing Station of Canadian C.F.A., will evacuate any casualties of 35th Division occurring before the reliefs are completed to the Field Ambulance of that Division at VERMAND. Tent Section, Canadian C.F.A will open at MONCHY-LAGACHE for treatment of sick of remainder of Canadian Cavalry Brigade, and will also collect sick from Div'l Ammn Column, Aux H.T. Company, Field Squadron R.E, at TERTRY, and from Div'l Supply Column.

MHOW.I.C.F.A.
Will stand fast and will collect and treat sick from remainder of Sec'bad and Ambala Brigades, Div'l Reserve Park, and Limbered Train, and will also be prepared to admit casualties from Advanced Dressing Station, Canadian C.F.A., and slight cases of Indian wounded from BOUVINCOURT.

3. Particulars regarding wells in the areas to be occupied and the amount of chlorination necessary are being issued separately to all concerned.

4. Route of evacuation of all other sick and wounded from Tent Sections of all Cav'y Field Ambulances of this Division as at present until further orders.

13th May 1917.

Brevet-Colonel, I.M.S.
A.D.M.S. 5th Cavalry Division.

Copy No. 1 .... O.C. Sec'bad I.C.F.A.
" " 2 .... O.C. Canadian C.F.A.
" " 3 .... O.C. Mhow I.C.F.A.
" " 4 .... O.C. Div'l Sanitary Section.
" " 5 .... "G" Branch.
" " 6 .... "Q" "
" " 7 .... C.R.H.A.
" " 8 .... A.D.M.S. 59th Division.
" " 9 .... " 35th "
" " 10 .... D.D.M.S. IIIrd Corps.
" " 11 .... " Cavalry Corps.
" " 12 .... A.D.M.S. 4th Cav'y Division.
Copies 13-16 War Diary.

A.D.M.S. 5TH CAVALRY DIVISION.

No............
Date............

No. 2232/17/1.

Copy No. ....

SECRET

G.O.C. Sec'bad Cavalry Brigade.
 "   Canadian   "   "
 "   Ambala   "   "

With reference to para 2 of this office No.2232/17, dated May 13th, from word "The" in line 3 to "established" in line 6 amend as follows:-
"The Tent Section will take over the 59th Divisional Main Dressing Station at St. CREN which is being vacated under orders of IIIrd Corps. Advanced party to arrive at noon on May 15th. All casualties from Advanced Dressing Station at JEANCOURT will be evacuated to St CREN which, subject to approval of D.D.M.S., Cavalry Corps, will become Main Dressing Station for this Division and for troops of 59th Division operating in conjunction with it.
For "BOUVINCOURT" where it appears in para 2 read "St CREN".

D. Macnab
Brevet-Colonel. I.M.S.
A.D.M.S. 5th Cavalry Division.

14th May 1917.

Copy No. 1..........O.C. Sec'bad I.C.F.A.
 "   "   2..........O.C. Canadian C.F.A.
 "   "   3..........O.C. Mhow I.C.F.A.
 "   "   4..........O.C. Sanitary Section.
 "   "   5..........5th Cav'y Division "G"
 "   "   6.............."   "   "   "Q"
 "   "   7..........C.R.H.A.
 "   "   8..........A.D.M.S. 59th Division.
 "   "   9.............."   35th   "
 "   " 10..........D.D.M.S. IIIrd Corps.
 "   " 11.............."   Cavalry Corps.
 "   " 12..........A.D.M.S. 4th Cav'y Division.
Copies 13-16 War Diary.

ROUTINE ORDERS (MEDICAL)
by
Brevet-Colonel.A.J.MACNAB.,F.R.C.S.,I.M.S.
A.D.M.S. 5th Cavalry Division.

11th MAY 1917.

----

64. HEALTH-SICK WASTAGE-SANITATION.
Though admissions to Cavalry Field Ambulances, and evacuations to other Hospitals, and to Casualty Clearing Stations during the past month compare very favourably with those of other formations, the period during which the greatest amount of sick is to be expected has yet to arrive. The importance of continuing to exercise the strictest sanitary supervision is again impressed on all Medical Officers. It is confidently expected that the care exercised by them in the past which has been with very few exceptions, most creditable, will lead only to redoubled effort now and in the future. Attention is again drawn to Fourth Army Routine Order No.846, a copy of which has been made available for all. Also to numerous instructions on Medical and Sanitary subjects, as they apply to Troops whether in billets, bivouac, or on the march, which have issued from time to time either from this office or from the "Q" Branch of the Division. No circulars or orders bearing on the subjects of Sanitation and prevention of disease are to be destroyed, but will be kept on a separate file, the production of which will be liable to be called for at inspections of Units. It is expected for instance that copies of this office Nos 5977, and 6340, dated August 26th, and September 18th 1916 respectively, will be found on the file.

65. TUBERCLE "CARRIERS".
Owing to the "combing out" of men for service there is a danger of old tubercular cases being sent to this country.
A case occurred recently of a man who had been suffering for several weeks from a cough being sent from the front to one of the Base Hospitals for a change. On examination his sputum was found to be teeming with tubercle bacilli.
In order, therefore, to prevent the spread of infection the sputum of all cases suffering from bronchial affections will, as far as possible, be examined bacteriologically. (D.G.M.S. D.G./D/ 393/13 "B".) (D.M.S. Fourth Army R.O.No.199).

66. CHANNEL OF COMMUNICATION.
A case has recently come to notice in which R.A.M.C. Officers have addressed reports based on work in their official capacity to the Medical Research Committee.
All such reports will be forwarded to this office for disposal (D.G.M.S. D.G./E/584/17). (D.M.S. Fourth Army R.O. No.201.)

67. "COURSES"-MEDICAL EXAMINATION BEFORE PROCEEDING ON.
It has been reported that parties sent to the Fourth Army Musketry School for a course have been found dirty and in some cases the subjects of scabies and other skin affections. All parties must be medically examined before leaving their Units.
The following extract from Fourth Army Circular No.G.S.318 (2nd Edition), Appendix 6, 5 (g), dated 8-1-1917, is published for information:-
(Medical inspection):-
" In order to prevent men being sent to the camp
"who are not fit to carry out the course,
"which entails a considerable amount of
"marching to and from the ranges, parties
"should be medically examined before leaving
"their Units.
(D.M.S. Fourth Army R.O. No.202)

68. ENTERIC GROUP "CARRIERS".
Officers in medical charge of Units will keep a careful watch of men who may be carriers of Dysentery, Paratyphoid or other organisms of the Enteric Group.

In the event of any man becoming suspected of being a carrier, as by repeated attacks of diarrhoea, or of contact with a succession of cases suggesting a possible casual relationship, the Officer in medical charge will report the circumstances to the A.D.M.S, who will arrange for the examination of the man suspected. Officers in medical charge of Corps Troops or Army Troops will report to the D.D.M.S., or D.M.S., as the case may be.

Men engaged in cooking or handling food when suffering from Diarrhoea are instructed to report sick immediately.

Such men should be relieved of those duties until they are perfectly cured and the Officer in medical charge is satisfied that they can safely resume them.
(D.M.S. Fourth Army R.O. No.194.)

69. TRANSFERS:-
Lieut N.B.AICH. I.M.S., (T.C.) SEC'BAD C.F.A., was transferred to Lucknow Cas; Clearg; Station, "A" Section, for duty on 7th May 1917. (Authority:- D.M.S. Fourth Army No. D.M. 3540, dated 6-5-17.).

70. LEAVE:-
Captain W.H.S.BURNEY, R.A.M.C., D.A.D.M.S., has been granted leave to the United Kingdom from 4th to 14th May 1917.

Captain J.K.CRUICKSHANK. R.A.M.C., (T.C), Medical Officer. 7th Dragoon Guards, has been granted 14 days' leave to the United Kingdom on renewal of contract from 5th to 19th May 1917.

71. APPOINTMENTS:-
Captain R.H.LEE, I.M.S., O.C. Divisional Sanitary Section has been appointed to carry out the duties of D.A.D.M.S., in addition to his other duties, during the absence of Captain.W.H.S.BURNEY. R.A.M.C. on leave.

72. ORDERS.:-
The attention of all concerned is invited to the following orders:-

Fourth Army R.O. No.912:- <u>SANITATION.</u>
" " " 913:- <u>SPECIAL HOSPITAL FOR SELF-INFLICTED WOUNDS.</u>

D.M.S., Fourth Army R.O. No.190:- <u>DENTAL ANAESTHETICS.</u>
" " " " 197:- <u>CORRESPONDENCE AND RETURNS:- DELAY TO.</u>

5th Cav'y Div'l Order No.1445:- <u>ABSENTEES.</u>
" " " " 1454:- <u>LOCAL AND TEMPORARY EMOLUMENTS OF SOLDIERS.</u>

CAPTAIN.I.M.S.
for, A.D.M.S., 5th CAVALRY DIVISION.

R O U T I N E   O R D E R S (MEDICAL)
by
Brevet-Colonel. A.J. MACNAB., F.R.C.S., I.M.S.

A.D.M.S., 5th Cavalry Division.

21st May 1917.

---

73. SANITATION.
The attention of all Medical Officers is drawn to paras 141-144, Chapter XIII, R.A.M.C. TRAINING.

74. INOCULATION.
Cases still continue to be reported in which Army Books 64 show no entries or incorrect entries.
It is essential that all Enteric Inoculations be recorded correctly in Army Book 64 and certified by the signature of a Medical Officer.

75. CORRESPONDENCE-CONDUCTING OF.
Much inconvenience is caused by the system in vogue at some Medical Units of submitting communications on two or more subjects in one memorandum. In a like manner references to various Routine Orders on diverse matters are oftimes the subjects of only one letter.
It is a cardinal rule of office routine that in correspondence, subject matters are not mixed or confused; consequently, one memo, or letter will deal only with one subject.
(D.M.S. Fourth Army R.O. No.225)

76. POLLUTION OF WATER SUPPLY.
Every source of water supply will be of the utmost value during the Summer months.
Preventive measures must be taken against pollution. The washing of clothes and the cleansing of all kinds of utensils, etc, in springs, streams and ponds, and in close proximity to well-heads, are prohibited. Ablution benches, baths, etc, are to be sited so that the waste water can be treated on land. Horse watering and washing are only to be carried out at the points provided for these purposes.
All ranks must be warned of the importance of these preventive measures.
(Fourth Army R.O. No.971.)

77. ULCERATIVE GINGIVITIS.
Ulcerative Gingivitis is a progressive inflammatory disease of the gums, and may also involve the surrounding tissues, viz. lips, tongue, hard and soft palate, cheeks and even the tonsils.
This condition commences as a cushion-like swelling, usually near a tooth. The gum on swelling separates from the tooth and later becomes discoloured with a yellowish-grey purulent exudate situated in the superficial layers of the mucous membrane. Deep to this exudate the tissues become necrotic, and very soon the infiltrated area becomes an ulcer.
To the floor of the ulcer adheres a yellowish-grey exudate, which, if removed, gives rise to free haemorrhage.
The ....

The disease is not to be confused with Pyorrhoea Alveolaris and is more frequently found in otherwise healthy mouths than in septic ones.

It is caused by infection with Spirechaetes, bacillus fusiformis and pyogenic cocci. "Vincent's Angina" and Ulcerative Gingivitis are identical in their Etiology.

The following methods of treatment are advocated:-

1. Hydrogen Peroxide and equal parts of Tinct of Aconite and Tinct of Iodine. Pack the pockets between the teeth with small plugs of cotton-wool soaked in full strength Hydrogen Peroxide. Leave them in position for ten minutes, then remove and thoroughly swab with the Aconite and Iodine. This should be carried out three times daily.

2. Frequent mouth-washes with a saturated solution of Thymol.

3. Let the patient rinse out his mouth with a warm mild Saline solution. The parts affected should then be swabbed with Fowler's Solution (Liq. Arsenicalis) by means of wool swabs held by forceps. Finally the mouth should be rinsed with warm water. Great care should be taken to prevent any of Fowler's Solution being swallowed. This treatment should be given two or three times daily.

(D.G.M.S., G.H.Q., No.C.667/93, dated 14-5-17.)

78. CEREBRO-SPINAL MENINGITIS-- BACTERIOLOGICAL EXAMINATION OF SUSPECTED CASES AND OF CONTACTS.

(a) Suspected cases will be sent to a Cas; Clearg; Station and the O.C. Cas; Clearg; Station will make arrangements for Bacteriological investigation.

(b) Close contacts of diagnosed cases will be isolated and a telegram sent by the A.D.M.S., of the Division concerned (by the D.D.M.S., in the case of Corps Troops) to the Officer i/c No. 10 Mobile (Bac) Laboratory informing Him of the location and number of these contacts. The Officer i/c Laboratory will proceed to the place indicated and will swab as many of the contacts as he considers necessary. After the visit of the Bacteriologist all contacts will be instructed to gargle their throat twice daily with a 1/5000 solution of Pot. Permang. in normal saline and at the same time to sniff this solution through the nose. The contacts should carry out this treatment under the supervision of a Medical Officer for fourteen days.

(D.M.S. Fourth Army R.O. No.216.)

79. SUPPLIES OF STRETCHERS AND BLANKETS.

Each Cas; Clearg; Station holds a reserve supply of stretchers. Officers Commanding Cav'y Field Ambulances requiring extra stretchers during operations will send an indent for the number required by any motor ambulance taking wounded to a Cas; Clearg; Station, and the stretchers will be despatched by means of the returning Ambulance. Additional blankets will be obtained in a similar manner if necessary.

80. The attention of all concerned is invited to the following orders:-

D.M.S. Fourth Army R.O. No.223:- ANTI-TETANIC SERUM.
Fourth Army R.O. No.970.:- LOSS OF MOTOR BICYCLES.

W. K. S. Burnley,
Captain. R.A.M.C.
for; A.D.M.S. 5th Cavalry Division.

ROUTINE ORDERS (MEDICAL)
by
Brevet-Colonel A.J.MACNAB., F.R.C.S., I.M.S.
A.D.M.S. 5th Cavalry Division.

23rd May 1917.

---

81. **MONTHLY SANITARY REPORTS.**
In future monthly sanitary reports rendered to this office will deal fully with the following points:-
(a) The sanitary condition of trenches and forward areas especially with regard to water supply, the protection of food and conservancy.
(b) The occurrence of infectious and preventible diseases, including scabies and infestation with lice, and the measures taken to deal with these.
(c) Arrangements for baths, disinfection and washing of clothing.
(d) Instruction in sanitation.
(e) The training and efficiency of the sanitary personnel of Units.
These reports must reach this office by the 25th of each month without fail.

82. **MEDICAL STORES.**
Complaints have been received from Medical Officers i/c Corps Troops that Cav'y Field Ambulances are refusing to issue them Medical Stores. Officers Commanding Medical Units will comply, without delay, with demands made by Medical Officers i/c Troops. In this connection attention is drawn to D.M.S., Fourth Army R.O. No.7, republished below.

" 7. **MEDICAL STORES.**
It has been found that individual Medical Officers have been in the habit of drawing drugs, etc, from the Advanced Depots of Medical Stores instead of from Field Ambulances or Cas; Clearg; Stations.
This practice will cease. All Officers in medical charge of troops must replenish their supplies from the nearest Field Ambulance or Cas; Clearg; Station."

83. **DEPARTURE:-**
23-5-17. Captain.L.E.Williams. R.A.M.C.(T.C.) to England on expiry of contract.

84. **POSTINGS; OFFICERS:-**
23-5-17. Captain.J.J.Wagner R.A.M.C.(S.R.) from Sec'bad I.C.F.A., to 5th (K.R.I.) Hussars for duty.

85. **ORDERS.**
The attention of all concerned is invited to the following orders:-
D.M.S. Fourth Army R.O.No.230;- EPILEPSY.
" " " " No.232;- FIELD MEDICAL CARDS.
Fourth Army R.O. No.,985;- MOTOR TRAFFIC PAST CAS; CLEARG; STATIONS.
" " " No. 992;- WATERING HORSES.
" " " No. 994;- PROTECTION OF WHEELS.
Cav'y Corps R.O. No.220;- LOCATION.
" No.221;- SANITATION.

W.B.Burnley
Captain.R.A.M.C.
for; A.D.M.S. 5th Cavalry Division.

ROUTINE ORDERS (MEDICAL)
by
Brevet-Colonel. A. J. MACNAB. F.R.C.S., I.M.S.
A.D.M.S. 5th Cavalry Division.

29th May. 1917.

---

86. WATER; PURIFICATION OF.
The attention of all Medical Officers is again drawn to the following extract from Fourth Army Circular No. 15, dated 17-8-16. This circular was distributed to all concerned on 21-8-16 and should still be in possession of Officers Comd'g Cav'y Field Ambulances and Regimental Medical Officers. If not the fact should be stated:-

X   X   X   X   X

"Where no water pipe line is near at hand Units in the trenches or those not in possession of water carts, should store the drinking water in 2-gallon petrol tins and the following procedure adopted:-
As a 2-gallon tin is equal to 1/50th volume of a water cart, the equivalent of 1/50th measure or measures of bleaching powder necessary for sterilizing the contents of a water cart should be added to each tin full of water.
Example:- If 1, 2 or 3 measures of bleaching powder are required to sterilize a water cart full of a given well water, then 1, 2 or 3 measures respectively of bleaching powder should be placed in one 2-gallon tin (stock tin marked "A"). This tin is then filled with the well water and thoroughly shaken. One third of a pint (6 2/3 ozs) of this concentrated solution from tin "A" should be added to each 2-gallon petrol tin full of water which can then be sent into the trenches or stored in billets. The water from these tins will be sterile in half-an-hour.

The stock solution (tin "A") should not be used after 24 hours.

Medical Officers should occasionally test the tins for free chlorine half-an-hour after the stock solution has been added in order to ensure that the stock solution is of the correct strength.

A (6 2/3 ozs) measure with a spout can be made of tin by any Divisional Supply Column Workshop.

Chlorinated water should not be stored longer than 48 hours."

X   X   X   X   X

87. SANITARY ORGANIZATION; REGIMENTAL UNITS.
The attention of all concerned is drawn to Field Service Regulations, Part 11, Chapter XI, para 84 re-published below:-

" 84. Regimental Sanitary Organization of Field Units.
I. The sanitary service of Field Units is organized upon the principle that every unit, through its commander, is responsible for its own sanitation and for the sanitary condition of any area which it may occupy. For this purpose each Unit is provided with

a.......

a Regimental Sanitary Detachment, as shown in War Establishments.

2. The Medical Officer of a Unit is responsible to its Commander for the efficient performance of the work of the Regimental Sanitary Detachment. The Commander is responsible that all ranks render a loyal and intelligent assistance to the Medical Officer in the performance of his Sanitary duties, and that the efficiency of the Unit is not impaired through neglect of or non-compliance with Sanitary rules.

3. The duties of the water supply personnel of the detachment are:
   i. The daily supervision of water supply, and its purification for drinking purposes by boiling, filtration, or the addition of chemicals, as may be directed.
   ii. To take charge of all apparatus and stores connected with the water supply of the Unit.

4. The duties of the Sanitary Personnel of the Detachment are, generally, to act as sanitary police in order to prevent soil pollution, and in detail, to supervise:-
   i. The preparation and care of latrines and urinals, including the filling in of the same, and marking of old sites.
   ii. The systematic collection, removal and disposal of refuse, by burning or other method.
   iii. The construction of ablution places and the disposal of waste water.
   iv. The sanitation of cooking places, horse and mule lines, and slaughtering places in the area occupied by the Unit."

88. ARTICLES SUBMITTED FOR PUBLICATION IN THE PRESS, i.e, THE MEDICAL JOURNAL.

It should be recognised that, as far as possible, the guiding principle should be that articles should not be put forward unless the matter is considered to be of practical value to the Profession generally, and of such importance that delay might re-act unfavourably on the treatment of sick and wounded. Articles so submitted must be passed to this office for submission to G.H.Q., in the first instance, whence, if considered of sufficient importance, they will be passed to the Press Censor for publication.

The journal or journals in which the author wishes the article to appear must always be stated. Articles must be written whenever possible, & submitted in duplicate .(Kings Regs. para 453). type-
(D.G.M.S.2218/240) (D.M.S. Fourth Army R.O. No.244)

89. DEPARTURE.
20-5-17:- Captain F.C.Clarke.C.A.M.C. 7th Canadian C.F.A., for duty with 4th Canadian Division.
(Authority D.G.M.S., G.H.Q. No.B.1478/48.)

90. ORDERS.:-
The attention of all concerned is invited to the following orders;-
D.M.S. Fourth Army R.O.:- No.237. PATIENTS KIT AND VALUABLES- DISPOSAL OF.
"   "   "   "   No.241:- DEATHS.
"   "   "   "   No.242:- INTERVIEWS WITH D.M.S. FOURTH ARMY.
"   "   "   "   No.243:- NOTIFICATION OF CASES OF SHELL GAS POISONING
5th Cav'y Div'l R.O. No.:-488:- ORDNANCE WORKSHOP; LOCATION OF.

W.H.B.Burney

Captain.R.A.M.C.
for; A.D.M.S. 5th Cavalry Division.

WAR DIARY
INTELLIGENCE SUMMARY

Army Form C. 2118.

(Summer XXXI)
1st to 30th June 1917.
A.D.M.S. 55th (2nd West Lancs.) Division

Place	Date	Hour	Summary of Events and Information	Remarks and references to Appendices
MOISLAINS FARM	June 28		Issued orders for move of Maintenance to SUEREBIE BERNES from STOREN, to arrange for hutments near STOREN on Rear Echelon for 4th Cavalry Division, from 4th & 5th Cavalry Divisions.	
	June 29		Recce — attend Corps & attend 4th Cav. divn at MONTIGNY FARM — inspected Aid Posts in position of line held by 1st corps — there Regt — of 5th Cav. divn were — up-4.5th. New Aid Post — in L33 to A.P. Regt No 30 — recon Horse Ambulance carrying arrangements, recce rear Aid Post, making arrangements with Traffic Control, to an MR. Traffic Control arrangements complete — there was a re-making of motor ambulance reporting line within —	
	June 30		Visited new recce arrangements completed — arrangements with Traffic Control at MR. hearts of — attended to from happy road bands, recce to within mR. Inspected hutments & — made ready— Infantry Camp 5th Divn, 9.5 Horse — p.5 division reported arriving in — within L — Officers Camp + matters within — recce — —	

WAR DIARY / INTELLIGENCE SUMMARY

Army Form C. 2118.

Place	Date	Hour	Summary of Events and Information	Remarks and references to Appendices
NORESCOURT FARM	June 5		Australian Brigade relieve Canadian Brigade in right Sector of line. Relief arrangements as in shewn Appendix I. Visited brain threshing pty in helier [?] wood.	
"	June 6		Visited threshing pty at JEANCOURT. Spent greater part of day in helier wood. P.B men et. removal carted in the area [illegible] been assessed expiring high - no importance to work.	
"	June 9		Can. by O.C 61st Dy. Battn. with Artsnts [?] recommended [?] country to E of Kern Horne W.R for an Atl A/R Portion & found suitable site in Collins Copse, were arrangements can be made for an 18' Elephant hut hq is L W fces of R recom N-N slope of Copse & see road went S on rd W of Arcannin Farm heres permanent plans for welfare arrangements for defm D of 12/13	
	10		Visited O.C Kern Horne W.R. Kerrnu he has seen & returned an Artes A/R Port. L.W. occupied to install p/R 12/13 [?] on Arthur Copse for new site. All Post to time his to N. O. 34.5: Power Horne 1st PAATAK. & Capt. the road in train.	
	11		ROBERTS Of te Atd Gineral Sti JEANCOURT & had him instructions re Southern threshing & Harvests review visits.	

WAR DIARY
INTELLIGENCE SUMMARY

Place	Date	Hour	Summary of Events and Information	Remarks and references to Appendices
MORESCOURT FARM	June 12		Visited G.O.C. See but Rh+ & explained relief arrangements for troops, & arrangements for evacuation & registration in coffins open.	
	June 13		Raid on Ascension Farm by 1/Spartans. Scheme have been kept when enemy: Casualties 1 R.O. missing, 2 R.O. wounded. 1 Indian O.R. wounded. 3 Indian O.R. killed, 4 wounded. 15 "	
	June 14		Relief arrangements have very well. + G.O.C. Bde + Brigade Bde acknowledged this. Stretcher bearers worked excellently + Brig 1st PNATAK is prompt answer to Capt Roberts on reaching HQ Post against nomethic war. Visited JEANCOURT & explained relief arrangements. Visited Colonial Bde at VERMAND + POEUILLY. Interviewed their M.O's brought to their notice from Bdes HQ the necessity precautions to found ...	
	June 15		Proceeded + Corps HQk to interview to Lieut-Col. A. April 14th. Promised report to have case - reported by A. Hunt. Visited Lucknow	

WAR DIARY
INTELLIGENCE SUMMARY
Army Form C. 2118.

Place	Date	Hour	Summary of Events and Information	Remarks and references to Appendices
NURLU COURT FARM	June 15		C.C.S. Experimental Battles at - VERMAND & POEUILLY. MNOW C.F.A. show Advanced Stunt. T.F.A. at - VADENCOURT & 9th Horse Lancers - Regt. reltive to the Int. Patrol in deep-recohi & our side Advance Troops of Cavalry. T.F.A. took over Int. Stunt. Pn at JEANCOURT. [illegible] arrangements as in Appendix No II attached	Appdx No II Op: Order No 18 Reform Pn
"	June 17		Proceeded to MG Australian Car Patrol & Conference on lumiere enterprise. Present Officers of various Arms + units on ground by G.O.C. Brigade.	
"	June 18		Proceeded to above Stunt. MNOW C.F.A. ex-VADENCOURT for to complete last night 10m 3.am. First Attacking Regt did Recce & formed up centre. Nature of enterprise was a Raid on St HELENS TRENCH by 9th Horse Train. Raid formed by 1/2 Squadron 8 Hussars + 1/2 Squadron 9th Lancers each in Firing Order & two horse respectively. All available Artillery in support	

WAR DIARY / INTELLIGENCE SUMMARY

Army Form C. 2118.

Place	Date	Hour	Summary of Events and Information	Remarks and references to Appendices
NOREUIL FARM	June 5		A considerable enemy attack & a number of casualties have been reported. A New Regtl Aid Posts were established at T road south of PT of PONTRU, and at the TWIN CRATERS. The normal Aid Post function section (Q numbers) became a loading post & rendezvous for stretcher bearers ambulances. From Advanced dressing Stn was at VADENCOURT. All casualties from north sector were passed to PONTRU (R.A.P. No 1) casualties from North guard on TWIN CRATERS (R.A.P. No 2) R.A.P No 2 constituted a Relay Post for No 1. At R.A.P. No 1 there M.O, 9 15 N.H. + an S.A. Surgeon. 8 A.B.C with 4 wheeled Carrier with stretcher attns. 8 spare stretchers & sufficient rehic equipment & comforts — first post think. At R.A.P No 2. M.O & 8 N.Numbers 8 A.B.C with 4 wheeled Carriers & two spare materiel & equipment in do do. At normal A.T. Post for Sectn (Current Numbers) 1 M.O & 8 A.B.C. 2 Horse Ambulances. 1 Jacht Car. Orders were given by this morning our A.T Posts across the rein—	

WAR DIARY
INTELLIGENCE SUMMARY

Place	Date	Hour	Summary of Events and Information	Remarks and references to Appendices
NURLU COURT FARM	June 18		Fired on by our own troops by mistake. Our casualties from this light - 1 B.O. slight wound, 1 other wound (serious). 1 B.O.R. serious wound. 6 /O.R. slight wound. 3 prisoners were brought in, 5 enemy bayonets + 10 bombs + 10 "P" bombs	
"	June 19		Went to see G.O.C. Canadian Bde who broke his leg entraining + spent the evening by a farm home to throw hand + having had permis= hire from his comments Arranged his evacuation to L'TINCOURT to Amiens.	
LE TOUQUET			Visited Canadian Artel ? training section les=NEUVCOURT. Draft orders for relief by Australn Bde by the Australns	
"	June 20		Instructions taken (Appendix No III of June 1917) Artillery lectures + inspection - Instructions to OC + forward on enemy attitude forwarded to Canadian Corps + howl troops on a situation Reproduced entente l'h Brigade + Div. Artillery	
"		21		
"		24		

Army Form C. 2118.

WAR DIARY
or
INTELLIGENCE SUMMARY.
(Erase heading not required.)

Place	Date	Hour	Summary of Events and Information	Remarks and references to Appendices
NOIRESCOURT FARM	June 25		Visited MIGOT & Canadian C.F.A in Track area, also Dort Camp Horse Station	
"	June 26		With D.A.D.V.S visited X Battery R.H.A, A.D.P. on of Stationers Horse. A resting R.C.H.A horse offers tonight. A.D.P. on in Quarry in R.H.C. Ands Present for in VADENCOURT.	
"	June 27		With C.R.E. to see D.O.C. sign-situation & ruinage from front Aid Posts in PONTRU to in sunken road to N. of TWIN CRATERS. Also saw spring water in grounds of VADENCOURT CHATEAU.	
"	June 29		With A.D.V.S to inspect horse dressing station, and advanced remounts station at VADENCOURT.	
"	June 30		Major A.C. RANKIN C.A.M.S. Arm was announced of Canadian Cavalry field Ambulance in his arrival from Cavalry Corps, relieves Lt Col D.P. RAPPELE who reports his departure to Canada tomorrow. To join 2nd Canadian Division. Freely is a stationer statuary numbers Adminsions to Hosp, Evacuation LT.C.S, & Return LT.Duty, & an return inclement reports.	

WAR DIARY or INTELLIGENCE SUMMARY

Army Form C. 2118.

Place	Date	Hour	Summary of Events and Information	Remarks and references to Appendices
NOBESCOURT FARM	June 30th			

	Admitted						Evacuated						To duty.				
	Officers		Other Ranks				Officers		Other Ranks				Officers		Other Ranks		
	Br	Ind	Br	Ind			Br	Ind	Br	Ind			Br	Ind	Br	Ind	
Sick	13	3	322	67			13	1	109	35			-	2	171	22	
Wounded	10	2	25	49			9	2	19	39			1	-	3	10	

Strength of Division British 7968
Indian 2799

From noon to noon
30th June 1917.

Signed
Colonel I.M.S.
A.D.M.S. 5th Cavalry Division

War Diary
Appendix No I
2 June 17

SECRET   Copy No.........

5TH CAVALRY DIVISION.
OPERATION ORDER (MEDICAL) No.6.

2nd June 1917.

Reference Map
$\frac{1}{40.000}$

1. As directed in 5th Cavalry Division Operation Order No.32, dated 31-5-17, the Ambala Cavalry Brigade will relieve the Canadian Cavalry Brigade in Sub-Sector A-1 on the night of the 5th/6th,- relief to be complete by 3.a.m.

2. (a) Any Units in and S.W. of VADENCOURT may be relieved during daylight on the 5th.
(b) Horses will not be taken beyond VERMAND in daylight, nor beyond VADENCOURT by night.

3. Consequent on and in accordance with above the Advanced Dressing Station, MHOW I.C.F.A., will relieve the Advanced Dressing Station, CANADIAN C.F.A., afternoon of JUNE 5th.

4. Arrangements for relief will be made direct between Officers Commanding, Cavalry Field Ambulances and their respective Brigades.

5. The 4 Wheeled Stretcher Carriers lent to Canadian Advanced Dressing Station will be handed over to the relieving Unit to which they belong at VADENCOURT. Care will be taken to hand these Carriers over clean, undamaged, and ready for immediate use. Any repair necessary will be undertaken forthwith.

6. All wheeled transport of the relieving Advanced Dressing Station, less one motor ambulance, will return to VERMAND, where one motor ambulance and one horsed ambulance will remain.

7. All casualties will be evacuated to the Main Dressing Station direct from Advanced Dressing Stations.
The Tent Sections of both Units will remain open for the reception and treatment of sick in their respective areas for the present. The instructions conveyed in this office No.2489/17 dated May 21st and No.2803/17, dated May 31st are again brought to notice.

8. Officer Commanding Canadian C.F.A., will detail one Medical Officer and twelve other ranks from the Advanced Dressing

Station....

Station of his Unit to report on being relieved to Officer Commanding, Main Dressing Station at Q.3.b.6.9.

9. ACKNOWLEDGE.

[signature]
Brevet-Colonel, I.M.S.
A.D.M.S. 5th Cavalry Division.

```
Copy No. 1....... O.C. MHOW I.C.F.A.
 "   "   2....... O.C. CANADIAN C.F.A.
 "   "   3....... O.C. SEC'BAD I.C.F.A.
 "   "   4....... O.C. A.D.S., Canadian C.F.A.
 "   "   5....... O.C. A.D.S., Sec'bad I.C.F.A.
 "   "   6....... A.D.M.S. 4th Cavalry Division.
 "   "   7....... Ambala Cavalry Brigade.
 "   "   8....... Canadian Cavalry Brigade.
 "   "   9....... Sec'bad Cavalry Brigade.
 "   "  10....... D.D.M.S., Cavalry Corps.
 "   "  11....... 5th Cavalry Division "Q"
 "   "  12....... 5th Cavalry Division "G"
 "   "  13....... 5th Cavalry Divisional Artillery.
 "   "  14-17.... War Diary.
```

S E C R E T.  No. 2968/17.

General Officer Commanding,
    AMBALA CAVALRY BRIGADE.

With reference to 5th Cavalry Division Operation Order No.32, dated May 31st 1917, the following Medical personnel, transport, and equipment, is at your disposal. Will you please issue the necessary instructions to all concerned, except to the Field Ambulance and Sanitary Section which are receiving orders direct:-

Medical Officers:-   Captain.J.J.Magner. RAMC, 8th Hussars.
                    Lieut S.Dutt IMS. 9th Hodson's Horse.

Orderlies for duty
with M.O's   :- 1 from 8th Hussars.
              1 from 9th Hodsons's Horse.

R.A.M.C. for water duties:- 2 B.O.R. from 8th Hussars.

Sub-Asst Surgeon:- from 18th Lancers.

Ward Orderlies :- 1 from 9th Hodson's Horse.
                1 from 18th Lancers.

Stretcher Bearers:- 24.:-
                8 from 8th Hussars.
                8 from 9th Hodson's Horse.
                8 from 18th Lancers.

For Sanitary duties :-
                2 B.O.R. from 8th Hussars.
                2.I.O.R. from Sanitary Section for
                each Indian Regt.

Batmen for Medical Officers:- 2.

T R A N S P O R T.

Two half G.S. Limbered wagons for Medical Equipment.

Two water carts complete:- 1 from Mhow I.C.F.A. now with
                                    Dismounted Reinforcements.
                            1 from Ambala Brigade.

E Q U I P M E N T

2 pairs Field Medical Panniers:- 1 pr from M.O. 8th Hussars.
                                        1 pr from M.O. 9th Horse.
2 Field Surgical Haversacks:- -------------do----------
2 Field Medical Companions:- -------------do----------
2 Haversacks, Shell Dressings:- -------------do----------
12 Field Stretchers:- from Mhow I.C.F.A.
50 Ammonia Capsules:- --------do--------

                                                                     P.T.O........

The Lance pattern Regimental stretcher will not be taken into the Line.

2. Advanced Dressing Station, Regimental Aid Posts:-

The Advanced Dressing Station of Mhow I.C.F.A., will take over the Advanced Dressing Station at VADENCOURT (R.16.a.9.4.) afternoon of June 5th.
Regimental Aid Post is at Cookers Quarry (R.11.a.8.4.).
An Advanced Regtl Aid Post at TWIN CRATERS (R.3.c.6.1.) is available when necessary.
The transport of all wounded unable to walk is by hand under Regimental arrangements from the line to Regt'l Aid Posts, thence by Bearer parties with Wheeled Carriers or by Horsed Ambulances after dark, to the Advanced Dressing Station.

3. Particulars regarding wells in the area being taken over and the amount of chlorination necessary are being issued separately to all concerned.

4. Ambala Brigade please acknowledge.

[signature]
Brevet-Colonel, I.M.S.
A.D.M.S. 5th Cavalry Division.

2-3-17.

Copy to.........O.C. MHOW.I.C.F.A.
Copy to.........O.C. CANADIAN.C.F.A.
"   "   .........O.C. SEC'BAD I.C.F.A.
"   "   .........O.C. A.D.S., Canadian C.F.A.
"   "   .........O.C. A.D.S. Sec'bad I.C.F.A.
"   "   .... A.D.M.S. 4th Cav'y Division.
"   "   .... Canadian Cav'y Brigade.
"   "   .... Sec'bad Cavalry Brigade.
"   "   .... D.D.M.S. Cav'y Corps.
"   "   .... 5th Cav'y Division "Q".
"   "   .... 5th Cav'y Division "G"
"   "   .... 5th Cav'y Divisional Artillery.
"   .... O.C. 5th Cav'y Divisional Sanitary Sec.

War Diary

SECRET.   Copy No. 10

Appendix No II
7 June 1917

5th CAVALRY DIVISION.

OPERATION ORDER (MEDICAL) No.7.

12th JUNE 1917.

Reference Map
$\frac{1}{40,000}$

1. As directed in 5th Cavalry Division Operation Order No.33, dated 9-6-17, the Canadian Cavalry Brigade will relieve the Sec'bad Cavalry Brigade in the Sub-Sector A-2 on the night June 14th/15th.

2. Following are Medical arrangements:-

   Medical Officers..........Captain W.J.E.Mingie.C.A.M.C.
                             Captain D.Murray C.A.M.C.

   Orderlies for duty with Medical
   Officers.................2 from R.C.Dragoons.
                            2   "   L.S.Horse.

   C.A.M.C. for water duties...2 attached to water cart
                                 furnished by Canadian C.F.A.
                               4 attached to water carts
                                 furnished by Canadian Bde.

   Sanitary Orderlies.........2 per Regiment.

   Stretcher Bearers.........24.:-
                            8 from R.C.Dragoons.
                            8   "   L.S.Horse.
                            8   "   F.G.Horse.

   #### TRANSPORT.

   Two half G.S.Limbered wagons for Medical Equipment.
   Three water carts complete.....1 from Canadian C.F.A.
                                  2   "   Canadian Brigade.

   #### EQUIPMENT.

   As in this office No.2232/17, dated 13-5-17, to Canadian Cavalry Brigade.

3. The Advanced Dressing Station, Canadian C.F.A., will take over the Advanced Dressing Station at JEANCOURT, on the morning of June 15th. Relief to be completed by noon. Four wheeled stretcher carriers will accompany the relieving Unit.

4. Of eight wheeled stretcher carriers now at the Advanced Dressing Station, JEANCOURT, four belonging to the Sec'bad C.F. will be handed over to the incoming Unit; four on loan from A.D.M.S. 4th Cavalry Division will accompany outgoing Unit and be returned to Sialkot C.F.A., clean and in good running order.

5............

5. Regimental Aid Posts are established at R.5.b.4.4., L.28.central (Quarry) and L.33.d.9.3. An Advanced Aid Post is about to be constructed in L.29.d.8.2. The Advanced Dressing Station is at JEANCOURT (L.26.d.2.0.), on which all Walking Wounded should be directed. All other casualties will be carried by hand from the Line to Regt'l Aid Post thence by Bearer party or by Horsed Ambulance after dark, to the Advanced Dressing Station. The Post at L.33.d.9.3. will be considered as a relay Post for the Regt'l Aid Post at R.5.b.4.4.

6. Two horsed and two motor ambulances will be located at MONTIGNY FARM.

7. All casualties from the Advanced Dressing Station will be evacuated to Main Dressing Station at the Sucrerie, BERNES (Q.4.a.0.7.).

8. Particulars regarding wells and water supply have already been indicated.

9. ACKNOWLEDGE.

Macnab.
Brevet-Colonel. I.M.S.
A.D.M.S. 5th Cavalry Division.

12-6-17.

Copy No. 1............ O.C. Canadian C.F.A.
Copy No. 2............ O.C. Sec'bad I.C.F.A.
"   "   3............ Canadian Cav'y Brigade.
"   "   4............ Sec'bad Cav'y Brigade.
"   "   5............ 5th Cav'y Division "G"
"   "   6............ "   "   "   "Q"
"   "   7............ "   "   "   Artillery.
"   "   8............ D.D.M.S. Cav'y Corps.
"   "   9............ A.D.M.S. 4th Cav'y Division.
"   "   10-12....... War Diary.

A. D. M. S. 5th Cav. Division

Appendix No III
2 June 1917

War Diary

SECRET.   Copy No. 12

G.O.C.   No.3373/17
SEC'BAD CAVALRY BRIGADE.   21st JUNE 1917.

Reference Map
$\frac{1}{20,000}$

1. With reference to 5th Cavalry Division Operation Order No.34, dated JUNE 20th 1917 the following Medical Personnel, transport, and equipment is at your disposal. Will you please issue the necessary instructions to all concerned except to the Field Ambulances and Sanitary Section which are receiving orders direct:-

Medical Officers:- Captain.R.C.P.Berryman.IMS, S.M.O.
                   Captain.J.N.Cruickshank R.A.M.C.

Orderlies for duty with Medical Officers:-
                   1 from 7th Dragoon Guards.
                   1 "   20th Deccan Horse.

R.A.M.C. for water duties:-
                   1 from 7th Dragoon Guards.

Sub-Asst-Surgeon:- from 34th Poona Horse.

Ward Orderlies:-   1 from 20th Deccan Horse.
                   1 from 34th Poona Horse.

Stretcher Bearers:- 24:-
                   8 from 7th Dragoon Guards.
                   8   " 20th Deccan Horse.
                   8   " 34th Poona Horse.

For Sanitary Duties:- 2.B.O.R., from 7th Dragoon Gds.
                      2.I.O.R., from Div'l Sanitary
                      Section for each Indian Regt.

Batmen for Medical Officers:- 2.

On completion of the relief the 2.I.O.R. from Sanitary Section now with 9th Hodsons Horse and 18th Lancers will be returned to their Unit.

TRANSPORT.

2 half G.S.Limbered wagons for Medical Equipment.
2 Water Carts complete:- 1 from MHOW I.C.F.A.(now with
                         Ambala Cav'y Brigade in the
                         line and which will stand
                         fast)
                         1 from Sec'bad Brigade.

Equipment............

EQUIPMENT.

2 pairs Field Medical Panniers:-	1 pair with M.O.7th D.Gds.
	1 " with M.O.20th Horse.
2 Field Surgical Haversacks...:-	do
2 Field Medical Companions...:-	do
2 Haversacks, Shell Dressings.:-	do

100 spare first Field Dressings.) will be supplied from
12 Field Stretchers.   ) A.D.S. MHOW I.C.F.A. To
50 Ammonia Capsules.   ) be handed over by Medical
) Officers of out-going to
) those of in-coming Units
) on relief.

The Lance pattern Regimental Stretcher will not be taken into the line.

2.   The Advanced Dressing Station of the MHOW I.C.F.A. now at VADENCOURT (R.13.a.9.4.) will stand fast.
Regimental Aid Posts are as follows:-
    Cookers Quarry (R.11.c.7.9.)
    A new Regimental Aid Post is in course of construction at FLEMINGS' CRATER (R.11.b.8.6.)
    When completed the evacuation of the Aid Post in Cookers' Quarry is contemplated.
Advanced Regimental Aid Posts for use as occasion requires are at Twin Craters (R.6.c.2.1.) and near T road to South of P of PONTRU (R.7.b.0.6.).

The transport of all wounded unable to walk is by hand under Regimental arrangements, from the line to Regimental Aid Posts, thence by Bearer party with wheeled carriers, or by horsed ambulances after dark, to the Advanced Dressing Station.

3.   Particulars regarding wells or springs in the area and the amount of chlorination necessary have already been issued.

4.   Sec'bad Cav'y Brigade,)
      Ambala   "   "   )
      Mhow I.C.F.A.   ) Please ACKNOWLEDGE.
      M.O. 7th Dragoon Guards.)
      M.O. 20th Deccan Horse.)

                              Brevet-Colonel.I.M.S.
                         A.D.M.S. 5th Cavalry Division.

Copy No.1...........Sec'bad Cav'y Brigade.
"   " 2...........Ambala   "   "
"   " 3...........Mhow I.C.F.A.
"   " 4...........A.D.S. Mhow I.C.F.A.
"   " 5...........M.O. 7th Dragoon Guards.
"   " 6...........M.O. 20th Deccan Horse.
"   " 7...........5th Cav'y Division "G"
"   " 8...........5th Cav'y Division "Q"
"   " 9...........5th Cavalry Div'l Artillery.
"   " 10..........D.D.M.S. Cav'y Corps.
"   " 11..........O.C. Div'l Sanitary Section.
"   " 12-14.......War Diary.

A.D.M.S. 5th Army Cav. Div.

July 1917

COMMITTEE FOR THE
MEDICAL HISTORY OF THE WAR
Date 16 OCT. 1917

Army Form C. 2118.

Volume XXII

WAR DIARY
or
INTELLIGENCE SUMMARY.
(Erase heading not required.)

1st to 31st July 1917.

Instructions regarding War Diaries and Intelligence Summaries are contained in F. S. Regs., Part II and the Staff Manual respectively. Title pages will be prepared in manuscript.

A.D.M.S. Eastern Dist

Remarks and references to Appendices

Place	Date	Hour	Summary of Events and Information
NOBESCOURT FARM	July 2		A.Asst. 34th Division appointed to arrange preliminaries for relief and handover of his area and takeover from Division was to be relieved by 3rd Division on July 3/4.
"		3	Proceeded to Cavalry Corps 10/30 to see D.A. &.S.
"		4	To see both M.R. line P.V.C. with regard to relieve arrangements for proposed operations 8 4 & 5th July. Owing to our heavy trench mortar preparations during the previous evening and our targets held by an enemy patrol outside the line blundering into our trenches, 2 Casualties. 1 O.R. 7h. 45. knocked & 2 O.R. 24th Poona Horse on right wounded.
"		5	The Division came into administrative command of 3rd Army on the departure of 4th Army from here. Also R.B. Bevan 67th D/B to Cavalry Corps for the month.
"		6	Orders for takeover of machine

WAR DIARY
or
INTELLIGENCE SUMMARY.
(Erase heading not required.)

Army Form C. 2118.

Place	Date	Hour	Summary of Events and Information	Remarks and references to Appendices
NUDESCOURT FARM	6		arrangements in regard to 7/8 July	
	7		drafted orders for methodical deployment, etc. 2 Bde L'Train. mines & recommended area of concentration of transition w/- O.C. Canadian C.F.A.; offr. staffing; D.M.O. Canadian Cav. Bde. June order 2 1/2 in armoured train armour Canadian	
	8		A trench raid by armoured train — bn half inflicted to 75 hanged Canadian I.O.R kiwed Canadian I.O.R. wounded Italian construction were still preceding about 30 C. Division mitra this april	
	"		At 9.10 pm preceded the Capt FAGAN RAMC & A.R.M. L- Regtl Aid Post on GRAHAMS POST. A very surprising & unsurprised raid on enemy trenches to enemy point south of BUISSON-BAULAINE FARM in Q.21.C and BELLEWLISE 1/20 was the result w- by Canadian Cavalry Brigade well carried out arrangements for evacuation, and emoluments of dead 3 wounded worked. Pa temps: Marshi from Collection Post L- Regtl Aid Post over 2 men guard, and that E	

WAR DIARY
or
INTELLIGENCE SUMMARY.
(Erase heading not required.)

Army Form C. 2118.

Place	Date	Hour	Summary of Events and Information	Remarks and references to Appendices
NOBESCOURT FARM	8		First casualty arrived in the Aid Post at 12.15 am. Poor not early lit 12.10. The question of transport was from Pack Horses. Arrangements at Aid Post were found to facilitate supplies, wounded were rapidly & well dealt with. By some principle Capt. W.J.E. MINGLE came to render every assistance to wounded. Ambulances in attendance on demand in Appendix transports the wounded, to being removed immediately. With casualties 1 British Other Rank killed " " wounded (slightly) 22 Other Ranks wounded 22 Other Ranks wounded & returned to duty including 1 Officer Thirty five prisoners were taken to Trenches FORT GARRY HORSE including thirty wounded. 2 Troops LORD STRATHCONAS HORSE One Troop SQUADRON Horse formed a Covering Party; the Currectany Post was established in vicinity of the house.	

WAR DIARY
INTELLIGENCE SUMMARY

Army Form C. 2118

Place	Date	Hour	Summary of Events and Information	Remarks and references to Appendices
NODESCOURT FARM	9th		Final orders for reliefs and moves of Cavalry Div. established on Division coming out of the line. The division will be relieved tonight by 36th Division & Div. units are now to proceed back into rear area. Div. HQ to move tomorrow to BOUVINCOURT	
BOUVINCOURT	10		Copy of a letter of appreciation of medical arrangements for Cavalry Div. from Canadian Corps and the loan of Field Ambulances and medical establishment generally from the Cavalry Corps and my reply forwarded to HQ concerned. Demand of appreciation of medical arrangements planned & executed, also receiving from officers of Canadian Brigade and external reference to Assembled medical officers of 13th Lancers with special reference to fracture treatment.	
BOUVINCOURT	11th		Inspected N.Z. manure. & Sphno. R.O.C. on mouvement	
"	12		Visited N/4 Canadian R.M. & though references necessity of informing men in sanitary condition of horses if we were to have Equine vit.	

WAR DIARY
or
INTELLIGENCE SUMMARY
(Erase heading not required.)

Army Form C. 2118.

Place	Date	Hour	Summary of Events and Information	Remarks and references to Appendices
BOUVINCOURT	12th		O.C. Field being left in temporary charge & orderly sanitary orders for the move northward. The train having been received	
	13th		Ambulance Pers. wrecked the morning. Section & Countries Pers. forward leaving : Convoy Field Ambulance accompany Pers. Operation order known on 9th & July 11th in charge. Distribution of Division areas in ST POL. Peronne B. & other in conjunction of Division areas as advanced by motor were impressed by ADMS & OC Sans Section & 2 hrs.	
ST POL	16		Arrival HQ left BOUVINCOURT for ST POL. Visits to note Hussumé C.C.S. at PÉRONNE LA CHAPELETTE to confer with O.C. in concerning the situation. Since has been army to the influx in to the forward areas of Indian Labour Battalions, impurities for adequate supervision of protection ag. the River, and the present medical arrangements have appeared that Army & Reserve withers to him general measures suggestions for final improvement. The situation in this is forwarded to one has increase the general health of persons troops	

Place	Date	Hour	Summary of Events and Information	Remarks and references to Appendices
ST POL	16		(a) Admissions are some of the suggestions made to ambulances is: (b) Concentration where possible. (c) Attention at himself Base for a [period] where urgent cases must be held. Their output uncertain, provision should be made for the extreme camp. The thermometer to have every opportunity to repeat [illeg] him the expected strain, from suspects. No further should be taken to front trenches - Bronchitis, Amyopneumonia, shin [illeg] [illeg] their own trenches, as Pneumonia. (d) Provision of transport rendering motor ambulances & stretcher accommodation from India.	
	7		Notes handing to recruits to determine location of MROW C.F.A. in respect of the must hand over O.C. or is Staff Length & arrangement for collection of British Sick Industries can be arranged. Personnel and at R-Romeo by Train.	
	19		Proceeded to Cavalry Corps HQ & offered various suggestions regarding proper maintenance of his [illeg] return to A.M. & Corps etc	

Army Form C. 2118

WAR DIARY
or
INTELLIGENCE SUMMARY.
(Erase heading not required.)

Instructions regarding War Diaries and Intelligence Summaries are contained in F. S. Regs., Part II. and the Staff Manual respectively. Title pages will be prepared in manuscript.

Place	Date	Hour	Summary of Events and Information	Remarks and references to Appendices
ST POL	July 19th		No movements for Corps on no Enfermerie L.I.O. evacuating to L/NB on interior. Strength [?] to County and M/NB	
"	20th		Returned to Anl M/NB	
"	21st		Visits M.N.O.W + Canadian C.F.A.	
"	22nd		Visits See but CFA	
"	25th		Proceeded to Corps M/S to interview officers [?] on bearing of Ambul Corps as has been in [?] seen July 15th in relation to censure	
"	26th		Proceed with Hastings to car upon strong 3rd Army at [?]	
"			ALBERT.	
"	29th		Inspected Park mounted section of Ambulance and MNOW Canty field ambulances.	
"	29th		Proceeded to Canadian Corps M/S to confer with officers.	
"	31st		Anl M/Q moved from ST POL to NEUCNIN a village some	
NEUCNIN			15 Kilometres to the NNW. The General Headqtrs the Division Service headquarters has been	

Army Form C. 2118.

WAR DIARY
or
INTELLIGENCE SUMMARY.
(Erase heading not required.)

Instructions regarding War Diaries and Intelligence Summaries are contained in F. S. Regs., Part II. and the Staff Manual respectively. Title pages will be prepared in manuscript.

Place	Date	Hour	Summary of Events and Information	Remarks and references to Appendices
NEUFVIN	July 31		Near Neufvin, continuing history of Indian Units	

Brigadier General Blunt J.a.2
A.D.M.S 7th Indy Division

A.D.M.S. 5th Cav. Div.

COMMITTEE FOR THE
MEDICAL HISTORY OF THE WAR
Date 16 OCT 1917

correspondence received.

General's Base Office.

ooOooo----

                            Date _____

	Case on which letter will be found		Initial of Reg...
	Main Head:	No.	

Army Form C. 2118.

WAR DIARY
INTELLIGENCE SUMMARY.
(Erase heading not required.)

ADMS 1st Canadian Division

Place	Date	Hour	Summary of Events and Information	Remarks and references to Appendices
NEUVILLE ST VAAST	Aug 1		heer ADMS Cavalry Corps re — St Michel sent nominal and numerical roll of him h horse O.F.S.A, Fie Nurse, Park horses to section & horsen ambulances of the unit	
			Arranged with Third Army & O.i.C no 12 Sanitary Section for Examination of Sanitary Establishments of men & Horse lines — Durance Etc	
	3		Park mounted Section See "Conf. O.F.S.A"	
	4		Conference of O.C. C.F.A & — Considered & Discussed principle & policy of hatters' arrangement to meet Sanitary arrangements etc — Chemistry & Action. Draft note of surveys. For discussion & underlying provisional considerations to gain amended renderings	
	5		D.A.D.M.S. inspected the Sanitary arrangements of 2', 7, 'D.G, '13th ' P.H. & found them satisfactory	
	7		A.D.M.S. left for England on 10 days leave	USAA
	10		D.A.D.M.S. inspected the Transport of M row C.F.A.	CHSA
	15		The Sanitary arrangements of Divison Hdg inspected & found satisfactory	W.USA

WAR DIARY
INTELLIGENCE SUMMARY

Army Form C. 2118.

Place	Date	Hour	Summary of Events and Information	Remarks and references to Appendices
HEU QRN	Aug. 18		Medical personnel for India Advanced Remount Depot, S.W.] BAILLEUL has been formed by 5a/Bad C.F.A. consisting of 1 M.O. 1 S.A.S. & 1 B.O.R. + 4 10.R. The strength of the Depot 3 B.O. 4 I.O. + 3 S.o. I.O.R.	W.R.A.
	Aug 20		Attends a Conference re opening Arrs. reqmts from leave	
	Aug 21		Preparation & Methods Rde returned M.H.O.W. C.F.A by ? Inspection General Coup Re Sanitation & hospitals etc	
			by D.D.A. Ambulances in district yesterday.	
	Aug 22		Attend Cavalry Corps + Arrs 4' Bar this moment & charma amusement seemy to Part-xviii her Epistles Lawsons	
		23	Inspects Lines, workshops & Sanitation J 34 '' Poona Horse	
		24	Inspects Lines, workshops & Sanitation J 7 '' Arequan Lancers	
		26	& Stationery stores Got inspection arrangement	
		27	& Cremation C.F.A. & Horse throughputs & See to Sanitary	
		29	Arrangement Attend cases.	
		30	Inspects lines, workrooms & Sanitation of Fort Percy Horse	

WAR DIARY or INTELLIGENCE SUMMARY

Army Form C. 2118.

Place	Date	Hour	Summary of Events and Information	Remarks and references to Appendices
NEUVILLY	Aug 31"		Major M. NOW C.F.A. Rome and arrived for consultation on case of Capt. M. MATTHEWS and interest his evacuation to No 12 Stat. Hosp — a hospital country arrangements for Canada & to Stat. Hosp mists to 12 Stat. Hosp and arranged for admission of Capt. MATTHEWS who has been by his consultant Surgeon III Army the several fever of his time. Some to work has been good. Re formerly Tutta ever number admitted to 2nd Ambulance. Evacuated to Stat. hosps & Returned to duty. Plus cases of Venereal Disease.	

	Admitted			Evacuated			To duty			Died
	Offn	O.R.	In.	Offn	O.R.	In.	Offn	O.R.	In.	
	6	1	206	27	9	—	116	27	—	94	15

Diarrhoea
Scabies
Venereal
People Part
Minor Parts P.U.O. &c

British 8 19 8 2
Indian — 1 1 8
58 8

COMMITTEE FOR THE
MEDICAL HISTORY OF THE WAR
Date 12 DEC. 1917

A.D.M.S. 5th Ind. Div.

WAR DIARY of INTELLIGENCE SUMMARY

A.D.M.S. 2nd Cavalry Division

Place	Date	Hour	Summary of Events and Information	Remarks
NEUVILLE ST POL	Sept 1		Cavalry Corps Horse Show was held near RAMECOURT S.#.9 ST POL in morning & evening. The Division won 5 2nd Prizes. Transport Competition, 7th Dragoon Guards. Signal Troop, Royal Horse Artillery. Officers Jumping with horses trained & broken by Unit, Canadian Cavalry Bde. Officers Chargers, officers Jumping, officers Jumping, Indian officers Chargers — Jemadar — 34th "Poona Horse"	
	Sept 3		Attended a Conference at 12 noon 7 April & W Army hqrs MH on C.F.A. & intervention an opinion on Reports of a higher standard of sanitation required on behalf of Cavalry Corps & on the 20th Indian Cav Bde. D.A.D.M.S visited 2017 Every Horse & Field Ambulance Stations. Commenced to examine & inspect Summers Clinic. The results were entirely satisfactory.	

Army Form C. 2118

WAR DIARY
or
INTELLIGENCE SUMMARY.
(Erase heading not required.)

Instructions regarding War Diaries and Intelligence Summaries are contained in F.S. Regs., Part II and the Staff Manual respectively. Title pages will be prepared in manuscript.

Place	Date	Hour	Summary of Events and Information	Remarks and references to Appendices
NEUVILLE	Sept 6		Visited Nile Supply Column & addressed all men of this unit who require re-inoculation with T.A.B vaccine or who are objectors to same. Been inoculated at once. The total strength of the unit has amounted to 1190 & the unit has had 107 refusals amounting to 17.2 times the amount of refusals representation was permanent. One reason of this is a permanent bad sanitary reason. As the department of this unit is a conscientious objector. Spoke to the supply truck on the subject.	
"	Sept 7		Inspected Reserve Park & addressed men of this unit who are supplying reserves inoculation. 12 or out I.I.G Strength 358. M/NGN in the two truck of the Knives.	
"	Sept 8		Lieut-Genl Sir H.V. Cox KCMG re inspects all Indian Troops in France including C.F.A on parade, afterwards the Indian Officers were introduced to him & Sergt Trent Sergeant in charge of Sanitation of R.A.I.C. Veterinary Section was	

2353 Wt. W2544/1454 700,000 5/15 D. D. & L. A.D.S.S./Forms/C. 2118.

WAR DIARY
INTELLIGENCE SUMMARY.
(Erase heading not required.)

Army Form C. 2118.

Place	Date	Hour	Summary of Events and Information	Remarks and references to Appendices
HEUCHIN	Sept 8		Inspecting of fields of manoeuvres & fixing suitable work place.	
"	Sept 9		Adherence men of the 3 & 4 A.C. Battery who report to the nominal reserves of heavy movements to [illegible] Batteries. 7th Army 3 arts of 11 coming & were moved to class to officers of the unit.	
"	Sept 10		Capt AMS Bonnay Blanc, Anjard, [illegible] (mornings) on 13 Hop [illegible]. Capt R.F. Fabian Blanc Princhet.	
"	Sept 11		Conducted inspections. L-GM innormal [illegible] regarding necessity of more regular & [illegible] inspections of British Batteries. Ask for the future. Arthenent deired that armies for more cooperation & assistance from officers [illegible] & [illegible] reserve in discovering of prevention.	
	Sept 12		Provence	
	14		Visited See. Gail. & Major G.F.M. Capt M.R. & see Attacks	
	17		Proceeded L-19/8 3rd Army for a Conference on Officer of Arms	
	18		To Cassel Corps HQ L-SSO Attack	

WAR DIARY
INTELLIGENCE SUMMARY
(Erase heading not required.)

Army Form C. 2118.

Instructions regarding War Diaries and Intelligence Summaries are contained in F.S. Regs., Part II. and the Staff Manual respectively. Title pages will be prepared in manuscript.

Place	Date	Hour	Summary of Events and Information	Remarks and references to Appendices
NEUVILLE	Sept 19		Inspected lines, anchorages, trucks & sanitary arrangements of Royal Canadian Dragoons & Canadian Mounted Rifles. Considered their management & for providing of twenty charges of clothing for men were inadequate. Arrangements for punishment of those unfit to speak Eng[lis]h	
"	21		Inspected Sec [No] C.F.A. & en route & similar point. Particulars to review the particulars	
"	22		Inspected anchorages, lines & sanitary arrangements of Civil [Reserve?] Column & D.X. Battery R.N.A.	
"	23		Inspected anchorages, lines & sanitary arrangements of N Battery	
"	25		Inspected lines, anchorages & sanitary arrangements J.O. Horses Park & Mun[iti]n Park & about C.F.A.	
"	26		Mobile [Cavalry?] Corps arrived J. in am. Accompanied him & in inspection of his [Division?] and [...] him the ordinary programme of two days routine had been reported & frame & C.O. in [Reserve?]	

WAR DIARY
INTELLIGENCE SUMMARY

Place	Date	Hour	Summary of Events and Information	Remarks and references to Appendices

NEUVCHAN
Sept 26

and Then an Transport has been sent out but on return
Rest chief & orders began being issued had been put in order
a temporary depot from the small Quartermaster Sect of Division
covering of this much hill in rear was also required ---
transport & regular overhauled. Notices with respect
next midst Question O.R.A. began has Transport but were
very nicely to article to equip near Rohrpost to men in leave but been
little no Care of Horses and multi-pumps help is necessarily
was noticed that wait --- home for this obviously is and
went with place in own

midn midst for hot G.O.A. train was in an urgent entirely
payment on rents to hand G.R.A. to attend his work
Sept 27 And in helping on extremely starting ...
Parade Open harness-Reins of M. O. O. Lt Ancher CFA
to attend them found on departures he by before
reports been to Transport lines & proper --- to be---in general

WAR DIARY

INTELLIGENCE SUMMARY

Place	Date	Hour	Summary of Events and Information	Remarks and references to Appendices
REVCN.CAMP			Did light place then others between amateur workmen of shirker previously reared by this unit. Air routes & duck are visible to keen dust smart assistants, example & instruction to pupils of Natal. A knowledge of horses, sham transmission to be kept. & advantage. Lunch in mess. Horse lines inspection & the horse inspection as. Saw a good & smart unit, turned out.	
"	Sept 28		Mr. A.D.M.S. Saw burials of an C.F.A. General condition satisfactory.	
"	30		Attended for transport N.C.O.s of Canadian C.F.A. & the shows. In Battery R.H.A. for a short course of instruction in British management an inspection to this. Saw a number men & Officers commd. to 5" Howitzers there & 18" Howitzers commd. by Officers brought to be unable to state numbers & command in his opinion in regard on seen.	Arrangements there by Lt. Col. St. Croy. Capn.

COMMITTEE FOR THE
MEDICAL HISTORY OF THE WAR
Date -8 FEB. 1918

A.D.M.S. 5th Can. D.D.

Oct. 1917

WAR DIARY or INTELLIGENCE SUMMARY

Army Form C. 2118.

1st to 31st October 1917.

Volume XXXV

Place	Date	Hour	Summary of Events and Information	Remarks and references to Appendices
HEUCHIN	Oct 1		Attended a Conference at Army. Visited HQ C.F.A. on return to Camp. Letters & hand mail from teams.	
"	Oct 2		The Major Genl Comdg. inspected No 1 Canadian C.F.A. and expressed a highly favourable opinion considering it an example of what a C.F.A. should be in every respect. He expects the transport lines of Canadian C.F.A. & the Divisional Train to match normal except that several inexperienced teams have had to be taken to Transport lines & it naturally takes a certain amount of training & shivering [?] to teach intricacies of methods, pack etc. Surroundings. Turn out of finish & if possible 10 vehicles & horses. Much can only be learnt by careful observation with C.F.E. My one 3 ton lot ammunition was APCR. Proceeded to Inspected Park in A Section Candhts C.F.A. Sutabich. Orders received for Divisional movement northward. Mapes [?]	
"	Oct 4		Orders received for Divisional movement northward.	
"	Oct 5		Medical Operation Order No 9 issued herewith	
"	Oct 6		Met ADMS Divisional General herein service in no. 12 statns	

WAR DIARY
or
INTELLIGENCE SUMMARY.

Place	Date	Hour	Summary of Events and Information	Remarks and references to Appendices
NEUVMIN	Oct 6		and offered suggestions regarding arrangements for Indian sick & casualties in new area. Proceeded to - Cavalry Corps H.Q. to report to A.D.M.S. Rouen 2. H.Q.r. 2nd Army to see Finds Hussain etc necessary information. Departed on return Canadian. See W.D. The named his movement. C.F.A. concerning hospital arrangements in that Line Ageing.	
NEUVMIN	Oct 7		Visit Ambula Post. from motorcars regarding transit of new H.Q. of C.F.A. left for Siril H.Q. at Poperinghe.	
POPERINGHE	8		Visited D.D.M.S. 2nd Anzac Corps & obtained in necessary information regarding medical arrangements. Visited 3 C.F.A's in Anzac Corps.	
	9		Called on D.O.M.S. XVIII Corps, and 2nd 2nd O'Brien 24 Army Corps 2. No 3 Canadian C.C.S. Remy Siding to see arrangements made for reception of Indian sick from the former Posts apart of 1 N.C.O. & 4 men in each of 2 Regtl Aid Posts in	
	10			

WAR DIARY
or
INTELLIGENCE SUMMARY.

Army Form C. 2118.

Place	Date	Hour	Summary of Events and Information	Remarks and references to Appendices
POPERINGHE	00/70		in lieu of POPERINGHE in care of Capt J. Rock & relieved as Secy(?). Capt. J.R. MASARD M.C. Rank of(?) C.F.A relieved Capt. J.A. MACLEAN on(?) replacement.	
"	12"		Visited MNOW & Sec but CFA. Arranged for 10 officers & Montreuse of stores for CFA & fur beats for Sec but & Creation of CFA 1". Smith ans(?) met to open & be accommodate suitable cases & to some ratings.	
"	13		Visited No 2 C.C.S OULTERSTEENE near BAILLEUL M/R & Canty(?) of Arrival Remount Depot, & of 5th Cavalry Divn Ammunition Reinforcements, transports into mutual arrangements. The Division in transit more Southward tomorrow Amsterdam Cantley Brigade 4th MNOW CFA & Art M&L marches b- RENESCURE area Sort of ST OMER. Sec. but & Canadian Canty Z Brigade with C.F.A attached move on 15th & 16th; respectively. Destination being area South of MONTREUIL. Snow(?) hour 17 & 18th.	

WAR DIARY or INTELLIGENCE SUMMARY

Army Form C. 2118.

Place	Date	Hour	Summary of Events and Information	Remarks and references to Appendices
RENESCURE		14th	The Division were materially other than Cavalry Corps. Visit Canadian C.F.A., No 3 Canadian C.C.S. at REMY SIDING. Saw Julian Sick and wounded up & re-investigated 16th. Visit also Aust. Second Army to report, & obtain information to lay before Cavalry Corps hors's arrangements. Also at Front Cavalry Corps to report.	
		15th	Orders regarding destribution of Division Generals Provost, Provost Marshall, FRUGES Area working HESDIN & East of MONTREUIL Country. Did Reconnaissance into Brigade Reserves Area. MTs at FRESSIN.	
FRESSIN		16th	Arrived with Aust. H.Qrs. Saw DD MS at RIYE on route & made suggestions for disposing of Ambulance. Brigade Train. etc & arranged 2- No SD C.C.S at—HESDIN which will be made into temporary War Hospital Unit. Submitted to Division Administrative arrangements for	
		17th	a Cavalry Pioneer Battalion Units in process to formation in BAILLEUL for employment in Second Army area. Visited M.I.O.M C.F.A. now open at CONTES. RHR Bde HQrs at	

WAR DIARY
or
INTELLIGENCE SUMMARY.

Army Form C. 2118.

Place	Date	Hour	Summary of Events and Information	Remarks and references to Appendices
FRESSIN	00/17		PLANQUES and See that CRA at FRUGES. Framer in situation of the smoking lesson of returning incoming recently to the troops in this area seeming receipt of supplies intended to compact keep Gutouris attention on nothing of local functions. Finished at 12m. these exercises troops order at 7.0 pm for medium personnel with equipment to proceed to join the Cavalry Princes Battalion in BAILLEUL tomorrow 18.	
"	00/18		Travened area occupied by Ambulance to see that RHQs, unit Ambulance AME supply, 185 horses, 8th Hussars, succession Powers sector Selhut C.F.A	
"	00/19		Visits Canadian C.F.A to impart instruction for him (processor) L. Rate Af pm Home & Ministry RHA and on L FRENCH, W.E. OC no 6 Staff Hosp, stated fact. 1 personal from L.horne CEG. had the discretion to omit most Indian sick from this Amer, and to the amounts	

Army Form C. 2118.

WAR DIARY
or
INTELLIGENCE SUMMARY.
(Erase heading not required.)

Place	Date	Hour	Summary of Events and Information	Remarks and references to Appendices
FRESSIN	00/20		Proceeded to 2 S.R.D. Hosp'l & interview drs & Div Army & O/C 15 mule Ambulance arrangements for Div. Late arr'l. Transport completed by Oct '24. The intern'l route to FREVENT this is 18 mile distant, from the MHOW C.F.A & CONTES and 26 mile from the SEC (a) C.F.A at FRUGES. Visited Canadian C.F.A & arrange for haulage required for sick this am formed - the must remaining there in hours. Visited Sec Ha'l C.F.A in barracks. She units are in segreg'l prem's - part of an Hospice at FRUGES but can ac commo'd 30 L.T.S. lives.	
"	21			
"	22		Visited & Matron North & inspected medical & cooking arrangements Inspected Hosp'l kitchen, bakehouse in 2 MHOW C.F.A all satisfactory.	
"	23		CONTES and found in ordere'l satisfactory. Inspected 'Spaston myth Northfield and Hosp'l at MARENLA (Sanitary kitchen arrangements) & formed much less - hin Latrine Instruction given to the medl Officer in charge.	

WAR DIARY or INTELLIGENCE SUMMARY

Army Form C. 2118.

Place	Date	Hour	Summary of Events and Information	Remarks and references to Appendices
FRESSIN	Oct. 23		In search of representation huts for the Bde & the Canadian C.F.A. moved from NEUVILLE those necessitating an inspection of BRIMEUX, Lichty, 6 km North from MONTREUIL on the MONTREUIL - HESDIN road.	
	24		Roger Church Argoon & Frencheim district visited	
	25		Spoken to inspected Canadian C.F.A. at BRIMEUX & found satisfactory approval necessary to form the settling and incommodation both for side, personnel & animals.	
	26		Proceeded to see huts 2nd Army at CASSEL. D.D.M.S. Canadian Corps at POPERINGHE and 5th Cavalry Division Battalions authorities VLAMERTINGHE & YPRES. Arranged for inspection of Instruction & Battalion by No 2 U.C.S. RAILHEUL himself.	
	27	10	J.F. Hinman M/Sm to obtain necessary information from Corp. J.J. MARNEE ROMC (S.R.) them in obtaining for a permanent commission.	

Army Form C. 2118.

WAR DIARY
or
INTELLIGENCE SUMMARY.
(Erase heading not required.)

Instructions regarding War Diaries and Intelligence Summaries are contained in F. S. Regs., Part II. and the Staff Manual respectively. Title pages will be prepared in manuscript.

Place	Date	Hour	Summary of Events and Information	Remarks and references to Appendices
FRESSIN	Oct 30		Proceeded to Corps HQRS to see Asst. Director Veterinary Services in Pommera regarding mobile Veterinary Sections. Rabies seems to protect regarding to severe. Numerous of use & parasitic mange & Rabies French to Indian remounts & horse. Corps Cavalry of II Anzac Corps became situated to the Station for Famine.	
	Oct 31		Received orders — Division Train moves to see and attached on march to Squadron moving to N° 2 Stationary Hospital, & Squadrons & 2 men Recessed to HQ. Others in rest of squadron & two cars allotted for Greenfield's Home.	

A. Hennessy Ln. Lt. Col. A.D. Ass. Director

Statement showing number of admissions to Cavalry Field Ambulances, number of evacuations, and number returned to duty during the month of October 1917.

	Admissions.	Evacuations.	To duty.	Remarks.
British.	213.*	160.**	53.***	* 132 from Canadian Cav:Bde.
				** 114 " "
				*** 15 " "
Indian.	61.	39.	20.	
Totals.	274.	199.	73.	

Average daily strength of Division for the month :-   British. 6606.   Indian. 2489.

Statement showing number of cases of Preventable Diseases admitted to Cavalry Field Ambulances during the month of OCTOBER 1917.

	British.	Indian.
DIARRHOEA.	3.	1.
SCABIES.	18.	3.
VENEREAL.	21.*	-
MUMPS.	-	1.
PNEUMONIA. (Lobar)	1.	-
MINOR FEVERS; P.U.O, etc.	21.	3.

* 20 cases from Canadian Cavalry Brigade.

COMMITTEE FOR THE
MEDICAL HISTORY OF THE WAR
Date -8 FEB. 1918

WAR DIARY / INTELLIGENCE SUMMARY

Army Form C. 2118

Volume XXXVI — Medical

A.D.M.S. 5th Canadian Division

1st–30th Nov 1917

Place	Date	Hour	Summary of Events and Information	Remarks and references to Appendices
FRESSIN	Nov 1st		Visited Major O.F.A., Canadian C.F.A. regarding the mortality rate ratios of Admissions & Evacuations in the Brigade. Attempt made; not met. Thick Doot-Serry Horse.	
	Nov 3rd		Assumed India & District Cavalry a/c known to absence of the permanent incumbent on 14 days leave.	
	Nov 5th		Proceeded to Cavalry A/P H/Qs. Visited Nos 6 Stationary, Prevent — en route to arrange further details re evacuation of India sick from the Division to Rouen to Richmond C.C.S. per arrangements in Cavalry a/c N/Up, in connection with the ratios & the drawing of rations for personnel & patients.	
	Nov 7th		The Division receives orders to move South. Australian and Sea Island Pile & Infantries area have - 5 Divisions on Feb 9 F. Canadian Rifle & Field Troops proceeding next day.	
	Nov 9th		Held Conference of Medical Officers of Canadian Cavalry Bde in Canadian G.O. with the object of informing the present situation proportional amount of Sickness & hospitals per ward in Army Bde.	

2353 Wt. W2544/1454 700,000 5/15 D.D.&L. A.D.S.S./Forms/C. 2118.

WAR DIARY
INTELLIGENCE SUMMARY

Army Form C.2118.

Place	Date	Hour	Summary of Events and Information	Remarks and references to Appendices
FRESSIN	Nov 8		Sent for the other two Brigades of the Division; instructed Commanding Officers (as head of other arrangements before O.C. Squadron tended to the nearer Officer), of more consideration in welfare relative to the provision of accommodation for men. Inspection Rooms & the sitting up of the C.F.A. (G) close attention to matter especially to health, cleanliness & of horses, & the provision of our private & any animal communication. The instruction to be himself in a satisfactory condition. Brigade on his return from leave found others that he assumed the C.F.A. & commanding area on the 17th of November.	
	Nov 9		Another see but Rlt. with C.F.A.	
			to OUTREBOIS area	
OUTREBOIS	Nov 10		Canadian Cavalry Brig. with C.F.A. & Divl Troops marched to OUTREBOIS area leaving Rules continued their march Southward. Report Centre & Divl H/Qrs at OUTREBOIS - OCCOCHES west of DOULLENS. Brigades - Canadian Cavalry Brig. H/Qrs at BEAUVOISNE & remained for tonight.	

WAR DIARY
of
INTELLIGENCE SUMMARY.
(Erase heading not required.)

Army Form C. 2118.

Place	Date	Hour	Summary of Events and Information	Remarks and references to Appendices
QUERRIEU	Nov 11"		Divl H/Qrs moved to QUERRIEU. The Division continues its march to an area east of PERONNE. An nursing instruction reporting evacuation of sick while on the march made nil. R.E.D. Ambulance.	
BOUVINCOURT	Nov 12"		Divl H/Qrs to BOUVINCOURT which offers ample accomm for Group. Ambulances see hospitals CARTIGNY & VRAINES area in horse on by night. MMOW C.F.A is in CARTIGNY. 2nd bn C.F.A at ESTRÉES-EN-CHAUSSÉES.	
"	Nov 13"		Visited MMOW & 2nd bn C.F.A. When home to ROISEL RLI affternoon. Proceeded to 4th Cav Divl H/Qrs to see A/Dms. Attended Cavalry Corps conference. Returned. Positions of Ambulances, personnel & equipment unsatisfactory. Remain Boltn, & Ambulances to No 2 C.C.S at OULTERSTEENE.	
"	Nov 14"		Cavalry Corps moved to VILLERS-CARBONNEL; received notification of conference of A/Dms's at office of A/Dms to Cavalry Corp. Third Divn personnel in his area. Inspected. Visited CARRETTE 2F.A & Sec' bn C.F.A at ROISEL, also 5 & 53" C.C.S at TINCOURT.	
"	Nov 15"		Attended a conference on H/Qrs 2 Cavalry Divn.	

WAR DIARY
INTELLIGENCE SUMMARY

Place	Date	Hour	Summary of Events and Information	Remarks and references to Appendices
BOUVINCOURT	Nov 16		Troops & inhabitants received instructions regarding gas/air Zepp raids & Regt'l relief system & Rail evacuations: Also met on 2522 held organization - minor report and Fair Act.	
"	Nov 17		At - MONCHY-LA-GACHE HQ - Arrived 2nd Cavalry Divn minor reports III Corps and obtaining am recovery in formation of divisions of infantry (M) Posts and street trenches. Ham R, II Corps Herein trench to be an advanced Base in Bouveau - trench line in - FINS + to be an advanced base in Boucly - COURT	
"	Nov 18		At AM Arrived orders received telling 2nd Cavalry M/Michel Arrived 2nd Cavalry Divn in enemy minor attack Cavalry Divn in enemy	
"	Nov 19		Held a Conference of O.C. C.F. A & S., O.C. base hounds Sections & Adm captains proposed medical arrangements & the further subdivisions of am immediate the division moved Adv HQrs to 2nd Advance were of am.	

WAR DIARY / INTELLIGENCE SUMMARY

Army Form C. 2118.

Place	Date	Hour	Summary of Events and Information	Remarks and references to Appendices
FINS	Nov 19		"MND" concentration N.E. of FINS.	
"	Nov 20		At Zero hour 6.20 a.m. attack began. Some 280 Tanks & Divns of Infantry only of the line formed up from in position Tanks going up without him — & (preceded by a creeping artillery barrage) — followed by Inf: over-ran to 5 mls ^ Havrincourt Trans ? Hindenburg line on whole front. Cavalry entered Masnieres about noon. 5th Cav. Div. reported to have reached Rumilly — Crevecoeur Sector — Attacked ? — Church Rifle Pits	
NE of VILLERS PLOUICH			VILLERS-PLOUICH by 3 p.m. Advanced of South at Masnieres reach to com Canal l'Escaut. See the with the Pas. Section at MARCOING. Anahala (?) Rgt. between VILLERS-PLOUICH & MARCOING in reserve. Medical arrangements — as per report attached.	
"	Nov 21		2 Squadrons 2 Lanark Yeomanry returning with walking wounded. Yesterday Various Squadron charged & from brittery. + Sethin ? read up to machine gun fire. Saltered 50%	

Army Form C. 2118.

WAR DIARY
INTELLIGENCE SUMMARY.
(Erase heading not required.)

Place	Date	Hour	Summary of Events and Information	Remarks and references to Appendices
N.E. of VILLERS PLOUICH	Nov 21		1. Gpnmelles, 1 Spratroups 7 - 4th, 5th NOYELLES sur L'ESCAUT. Total Casualties Provisions 7 - 2 Officers in an has attached report. The Division stood to in the day	
EQUAN COURT	Nov 22		The Division (relieved) at 10.30 am 4 - FINS	
SUZANNE	Nov 23		The Division moved West - to BRAY	
MONCAY LA GACHE	Nov 27	15	The Division marched 4 - area E. of PERONNE. Reports 2 - attack in north- and received his appreciation of recent enemy movements have been received operations of Divisions report before 17th Apric a No 4 - major Genl Connell will be Relief courage and courage and confidence. See Para on "TREFCON, Canadians an MAONI 4 - GERTET, MERAUCOURT.	
"	Nov 28		Total wounded of the Division from 20th - 28th inclusive amounts to 6 Officers + 56 other ranks distribute as follows	

Army Form C. 2118.

WAR DIARY
or
INTELLIGENCE SUMMARY.
(Erase heading not required.)

Instructions regarding War Diaries and Intelligence Summaries are contained in F. S. Regs., Part II and the Staff Manual respectively. Title pages will be prepared in manuscript.

Place	Date	Hour	Summary of Events and Information	Remarks and references to Appendices
MONCHY-LA-CACHE	28th		Officers: 4th Dragoon Guards. 2/Lt GILMAN. R.S. G.S.W. Thigh. L. Severe. 1st Cavy Horse. Major SHARPE. G.S.W. Knee. Slight. 1st Cavy Horse. Lieut. COHEN. W.H. G.S.W. Neck. Severe. Fort Garry Horse. Lieut. HOLIDAY. P.M. G.S.W. Knee. Slight. Lord Strathcona Horse. Lt.Col. DOCHERTY. M. G.S.W. Shoulder R. Rejoined Unit 22-11-14. C.A.N.E. att R.C.D. Capt. MINGIE. M.T.E. G.S.W. Hand R. Rejoined Unit 24-11-14. OTHER RANKS: Fort Garry Horse. 29. Lord Strathcona Horse. 9. 4th Dragoon Guards. 3. H.Q. Canadian Cav. Bde. 1. Canadian M.G. Squadron. 2. 1st Bde RHA Ammn. Col. 1. Royal Canadian H.A. 2. 2nd Dragoon Horse. 1. Royal Canadian Dragoons. 5. 13th M.G. Squadron. 4.	

WAR DIARY or INTELLIGENCE SUMMARY

Army Form C. 2118.

Place	Date	Hour	Summary of Events and Information	Remarks and references to Appendices
MONCHY LA GACHE	Mar 29		Proceeded to 14th Lp Cavalry Corps for arrangements regarding motor ambulance arrangements for wounded. This was a continuation of the plan approved in MIGNON RANCH 2 - a rand trick farm rehearsing the 24th division (infty) on Dec 17.	
R.S. at KER-d ERÉNY	Mar 30		The division moved at very short notice this morning. A Mobile R.S. was established MH unit Off. A. Pension for VILLERS-FAUCON. Went on of a less Park with certain 4 horse ambulances of MIGON OF A have extended to 2 Bearer divisions. 2 SMO L 72 men were placed in attendance. I retired to division on arrival in their Report centre the rest of the division became evident. My hit of ambulances repaired of mysterious enemy wounded struck in Roads, & determined in advance on the GOUZEAUCOURT - FINS Road - Sharp however in the open; withdrew Bearer party from M.D.S. at VILLERS-FAUCON	

WAR DIARY
or
INTELLIGENCE SUMMARY.

Army Form C. 2118.

Place	Date	Hour	Summary of Events and Information	Remarks and references to Appendices
R S W HQ N I Septmr	Nov 30		and having through D.A.D.M.S obtained known note - O.C. MMOW C.F.A informed him — letter from him with leaving Bgd and valuable information regarding his position & his Row of ammunition decided to remain on NEUDICOURT. FINS in the evening returning for an instant of the division. Sent D.A.D.M.S to VILLERS-FAUCON AM & arranged Motor Officer 2 (15 Horses in a Signals Pure Car L. Avise WB 2 FORD Ambulance & a spare Bgd Bearer L. Avenue Report — Conform on his return at 11 pm ordered an available Bearers & start G.E.A L. return — home in person Apr'd Set Sect & Ambulance proceed L. KRn. Rte 14½D to O.C. & Ambulance and to give instructions	Signed [signature] Stuff S.T. Cr. Div

SECRET.

Copy No... 12

5th CAVALRY DIVISION.
OPERATION ORDER (MEDICAL) No.11.

8th November 1917.

Reference Map 1/100,000, Sheet LENS 11.

1. The Division will move South on November 9th and 10th.

2. Field Ambulances will march and billet under orders of the Brigade to which they are attached.

3. Motor Ambulances will be at the disposal of Officers Commanding, Cavalry Field Ambulances who will ensure that they move to their destination in such a manner as not to interfere with troops on the march.

4. Sanitary Section will move with the Supply Column.

5. Officer Commanding, Canadian C.F.A., will detail an Officer for Medical charge of the Dismounted Reinforcements. He will report to O.C., Dismounted Reinforcements at WANIN tomorrow the 9th inst. A motor ambulance will be placed at his disposal by the Unit to which he belongs. While in this area he will evacuate British sick to No. 59. Cas: Clrg: Station, HESDIN. Indian sick to No. 6. Stationary Hospital, FREVENT. Officer Commanding, Sec'bad I.C.F.A., will detail a Ward Orderly to assist the Medical Officer, Dismounted Reinforcements. Names of Medical Officer and Ward Orderly selected will be furnished to this office forthwith.

6. Following are arrangements for evacuation of sick:-

OUTREBOIS area:- British ranks to No.3.Canadian Stationary Hospital, DOULLENS.

Indian ranks to No. 6. Stationary Hospital, FREVENT.

CONTAY area:- British ranks to No.50. Cas: Clrg: Station, EDGEHILL.

Indian ranks to Lucknow Cas: Clrg: Station at PERONNE-LA-CHAPELETTE.

7. Reports to FRESSIN up to 11.a.m, 10th inst. Later location of Report Centre will be notified. Daily States to reach this office by 10-30.a,m, daily.

8. ACKNOWLEDGE.

Macnab
COLONEL.I.M.S.
A.D.M.S.,5th Cavalry Division.

Copy No.1.....O.C.,Canadian C.F.A.   No.8. D.D.M.S., Cav Corps.
"   No.2.....O.C. Sec'bad I.C.F.A.   No.9. Canadian Brigade.
"   No.3.....O.C.,Lhow I.C.F.A.   No.10.Sec'bad   "
"   No.4.....O.C.,Sanitary Section. No.11. Ambala   "
"   No.5.....5th Cavalry Division "Q" No.12-14. War Diary.
"   No.6.....5th Cavalry Division "G"
"   No.7.....O.C. Dismounted Reinforcements.

SECRET.

Copy No. 25

5th CAVALRY DIVISION.

OPERATION ORDER (MEDICAL) No.12.

A.D.M.S.
5TH
CAVALRY DIVISION.

18th November 1917.

Reference Map,
1/40,000.

1. In accordance with instructions received the Division (less "B" Echelon, Sanitary Section, A.H.T.Coy, Heavy Section, Reserve Park and Dismounted Reinforcements) will march to a Forward Concentration Area, N.E. of FINS on Y/Z night in accordance with a march table which will be issued later.
    The Grouping for this move and the subsequent forward moves of the Division is shown in Appendix "A" attached.

2. In moving to the Forward Concentration Area, whereever possible, squadrons will move off the roads. All wheels will move by the roads only. Squadrons and wheels will move closed up.

3. On arrival in the Forward Concentration Area there will be a halt of two and a half hours during which horses will be watered and fed.
    After feeding, nosebags will be refilled from forage dumps which have been prepared in this area.
    Arrangements will be made by Brigades and O's C. Divisional Troops for a hot meal to be ready for the men in this area.

4. The Division will be ready to move forward from the FINS area at ZERO plus 2½ hours.

5. Brigades and O's C. Divisional Troops will arrange for guides to meet Units at NURLU and direct them to their places in the FINS area.

6. WATER:- in area N.E. of FINS:-

    Brigade Point at V.6.d.6.7.) all on East of road
    "   "   " W.1.a.1.8.) from
    "   "   " Q.31.c.2.2.) FINS-METZ.

    Each point is capable of watering 2,500 horses in one hour. Troughs must be used from both sides simultaneously. Fences with "IN" and "OUT" notices will be prepared. Good policing is essential and each Brigade will send forward 1 Officer and 6 men to superintend watering.

7. Pack Mounted Sections will move from present area to Forward Concentration Area with their respective Brigades.

8. Field Ambulances, less Pack Mounted Sections, and less any G.S.Wagons of Tent Division so immobilized will move together. Their position in column of Route is indicated in Appendix "A", Canadian C.F.A., leading, 1how I.C.F.A., in rear.

9. G.S. Wagons temporarily immobilized in present area will be brought up to the Forward Concentration Area as soon as possible, and the teams sent back for this purpose should return with the wagons not later than ZERO plus 1.

10.............

10. Heavy Sections of Cavalry Field Ambulances will remain concentrated at FINS. Medical Officers in command of these Sections will be available for employment at IIIrd Corps Main Dressing Station at V.18.c.6.7. on FINS-NURLU Road, or for assistance in evacuating the Unit. Light Sections will move forward with No.2. "A" Echelons of Brigades.

11. A Bearer party consisting of 1 Officer from Mhow and Canadian Cavalry Field Ambulances and 24 other ranks from each Cavalry Field Ambulance respectively with 12 stretchers and all available Wheeled Carriers will be conveyed by motor ambulances to VILLERS-PLOUICH. The convoy will leave FINS at ZERO hour plus 1. From this point each party will, as soon as the three Brigades of the Division have passed, move on RUMILLY where a Divisional Dressing Station and Collecting Post for Walking Wounded will be formed from which Bearer parties will be available for the collection of wounded under the orders of the Officer Commanding. The motors conveying the party will be so parked at VILLERS-PLOUICH as to avoid any interference with traffic, and will be utilised for the evacuation of casualties when circumstances permit

12. Ambulance transport moving with No.2."A" Echelon will rendezvous at RUMILLY as soon as conditions allow. The motor ambulances previously left at VILLERS-PLOUICH will be utilised to evacuate from RUMILLY to IIIrd Corps Main Dressing Station.

13. Instructions regarding the duties in action of Regimental Medical Officers, Officers Commanding, Cavalry Field Ambulances, and of the Pack Mounted Sections have already been indicated.

14. Advanced Dressing Stations and Regimental Aid Posts in the Infantry Area are as under:-

Reference Map 1/40,000, Sheet 57.C.

20th DIVISION.

Regimental Aid Posts........R.20.a.2.9. (XVI Ravine)
R.25.d.4.9.

Relay Posts................R.25.a.8.4. (Hotel Cecil)
R.19.d.3.7. (nearXV Ravine)

Advanced Dressing Station...GOUZEAUCOURT. Q.36.d.6.9.

After ZERO hour others will be established at R.20.a.5.9. and at R.26.c.4.9.

Walking Wounded Station.....GOUZEAUCOURT. Q.36.b.1.4.

At ZERO hour Advanced Regimental Aid Posts will be opened at:-
R.20.d.7.4. and R.14.a.8.9.

12th DIVISION.

Regimental Aid Posts.......R.23.d.7.1. R.33.b.8.5. R.34.c.3.9.
(Cheshire Quarry)

Advanced Dressing Station...VILLERS-GUISLAINS. X.9.a.3.4.

6th DIVISION.

Regimental Aid Posts.......BEAUCAMP.) Map reference not
VILLERS-PLOUICH) available.

Advanced........

Advanced Dressing Station......Q.30.b.2.8.

IIIrd Corps Main Dressing Station and Collecting Post for Walking Wounded is at V.18.c.0.7. on FINS-NURLU Road.

15. <u>ACKNOWLEDGE</u>.

A.J.Maan&t.
COLONEL .I.M.S.
A.D.M.S., 5th Cavalry Division.

Copy No.1......O.C. Canadian C.F.A.
" " 2......O.C. Sec'bad I.C.F.A.
" " 3......O.C., Mhow I.C.F.A.
" " 4......O.C. Sanitary Section.
Copies No.5-16..Regimental Medical Officers.
Copy No.17.....Canadian Cavalry Brigade.
" " 18.....Sec'bad " "
" " 19.....Ambala " "
" " 20.....D.D.M.S.,Cavalry Corps.
" " 21.....D.D.M.S. IIIrd Corps.
" " 22.....A.D.M.S.,2nd Cavalry Division.
" " 23.....5th Cavalry Division "G"
" " 24.....5th Cavalry Division "Q"
Copies " 25-27..War Diary

APPENDIX "A".

GROUPING FOR FORWARD MOVE.

CANADIAN CAVALRY BRIGADE GROUP.

Canadian Cavalry Brigade.
"B" Battery R.C.H.A.
1.Field Troop R.E.
M.G.Battery.
1.Light Section Ammunition Column.
Pack Section, Canadian Cav Field Ambulance.

SEC'BAD CAVALRY BRIGADE GROUP.

Sec'bad Cavalry Brigade.
"N" Battery R.H.A.
1.Light Section, Ammunition Column.
1.Field Troop.R.E.
Pack Section, Sec'bad Cav Field Ambulance.

DIVISIONAL HEADQUARTERS GROUP.

Groups I, II, and III.
5th Signal Squadron.
Headqrs 17th Bde R.H.A., and R.C.H.A., Brigade.
2 Troops, Yorkshire Dragoons.

AMBALA CAVALRY BRIGADE GROUP.

Ambala Cavalry Brigade.
"A" Battery R.C.H.A.
5th Field Squadron less 2 Troops.
1.Light Section, Ammunition Coulmn.
Pack Section, Mhow Cav Field Ambulance.

No.1."A" ECHELON GROUP.

O.C.-Lieut.G.R.H.BENNETT. Fort Garry Horse.
No.1."A" Echelon Canadian Cavalry Brigade.Group.
 "   "   "   Sec'bad   "   "
 "   "   "   Divisional Headquarters Group.
 "   "   "   Ambala Cavalry Brigade Group.

No.2."A" ECHELON GROUP.

O.C.-Captain. & Qr.Mr.A.HIATT, 7th Dragoon Guards.

No.2."A" Echelon Canadian Cavalry Brigade Group.
 "   "   "   Sec'bad   "   "
 "   "   "   Divisional Headquarters "
 "   "   "   Ambala Cavalry Brigade "

CAVALRY FIELD AMBULANCE GROUP.

Canadian Cavalry Field Ambulance (less Pack Section)
Sec'bad Cavalry Field Ambulance (less Pack Section)
Mhow Cavalry Field Ambulance (less Pack Section)

17th Brigade R.H.A. Ammunition Column. (less Light Sections)
R.C.H.A. Brigade Ammunition Column (less Light Section.)
Reserve Park (less Light Sections)

No.5812/17.
****

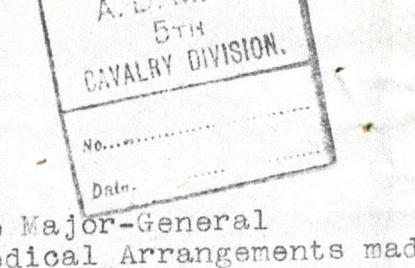

General Staff,
    5th Cavalry Division.

       I forward for the information of the Major-General Commanding, the following brief account of Medical Arrangements made and of orders issued by me during the recent operations together with an extract from a letter from the D.D.M.S., Cavalry Corps to whom the report was originally addressed.

2.   The equipment referred to in para 1 is that suggested by the Officer Commanding, of a Field Ambulance in the 1st Cavalry Division to whom the credit for it is due. It enables a Regimental Medical Officer and his establishment to attend to about 200 casualties independently of other assistance.

3.   I desire to acknowledge that it is owing to the information and assistance afforded me by the Major-General Commanding, and the General Staff that it was possible to evolve a plan of action for the Medical Services which seemed likely to meet the situation; and to say further that though the scheme was satisfactory as far as it went, it is realised that the real difficulties still remained to be faced as they came into view, and these one was prepared to meet as the situation demanded and as best one could.

4.   The conduct of the Medical Officer, Fort Garry Horse, has already been brought to notice and I desire to add that the Officer Commanding, Canadian C.F.A., showed a clear appreciation of his duties, and like other Field Ambulances of the Division was in a position to do more if so required.

                                   (sd) A.J.MACNAB.
                                          Colonel.I.M.S.
                          A.D.M.S.,5th Cavalry Division.

28-11-17.

Extract from a D/O letter dated 26th November 1917 from
D.D.M.S., Cavalry Corps, to A.D.M.S., 5th Cavalry Division.
****

"Many thanks for your most interesting report. I think your arrangements were perfect. The Corps Commander questioned me about the recovery of wounded of Fort Garry Horse. I informed him that you had assured me that all that it was possible to bring in had been **recovered** but of course I knew nothing of the details of the affair."

  x x x x x x x

No.518/M.

D.D.M.S.,
    Cavalry Corps.

         The following brief account of Medical Arrangements made and of orders issued by me prior to and during the advance of the Division on November 20th is furnished for your information.

1.   Immediately on receiving warning of a probable move forward from rear area of Concentration at BOUVINCOURT all Regimental Medical Officers and their establishments were equipped in accordance with the suggestions contained in Notes on Equipment of Regimental Medical Officers forwarded under your No.M/313, dated 7-10-17.

2.   A Conference of Officers Commanding, Cavalry Field Ambulances and Officers Commanding, Pack Mounted Sections was held on the morning of Y day when the whole scheme was explained in detail and my intentions as regards the dispositions of heavy and light Sections of Cavalry Field Ambulances, the formation of a Bearer Division, and a Section of a Motor Ambulance Convoy from the Motor Ambulances available were made clear.

3.   Instructions had previously been issued as to the methods of inter-communication to be adpoted and the ~~xxxxxxxxxxxxxxxxxxxxxxx xxxxxxxx~~ places to be assumed by Regimental Medical Officers, Pack Mounted Sections, and Officers Commanding, Cavalry Field Ambulances respectively.
(NOTE:- As an additional means of liaison experience having proved
         that roads are likely to be impassable for motor-cyclists
         it is intended on a future occasion to attach 2 Regimental
         Stretcher Bearers to each O.C.,C.F.A., as gallopers)

4.   The attached Medical Instructions were incorporated in the Preliminary Operation Order issued by the General Staff.

5.   On arrival at the Forward Concentration Area at FINS, (a) Heavy Sections, C.F.A's were assembled and ordered to stand fast, the whole under 1 Medical Officer with Sergeant Majors and Transport Conductors of each Unit to assist him. The services of the Medical Officer were placed at the disposal of the O.C.IIIrd Corps, Main Dressing Station at FINS.
(b) Pack Mounted Sections had already been attached to Brigades.
(c) Light Sections, C.F.A.'s were with A.2. Echelon of Brigades.
(d) Motor Ambulances of all C.F.A.'s with a Bearer Division of 2 Medical Officers and 72 Other ranks including 2 General duty orderlies as clerks were at my disposal.

6.   On ZERO day November 20th Bearer Division and all motor Ambulances were ordered to move to Western edge of VILLERS-PLOUICH at ZERO hour plus 1. Permission for the move had previously been obtianed by telephone from D.D.M.S.,IIIrd Corps. The party was visited by me accompanied by D.A.D.M.S., at 8.p.m, and found correct.

7.   Morning of 21st Bearer Division with all Motor Ambulances was advanced to a point abreast of Divisional Report Centre at R.9.b.8.8. and all cars lined up on right of VILLERS-PLOUICH-MARCOING road heading West. On arrival a stretcher bearer party was at once sent forward to a Relay Post near Marcoing whence 1 Officer and 14 other ranks belonging to Units of 29th Division all lying cases whose position had been reported to me by the O.C.,Sec'bad I.C.F.A. were hand carried to motor ambulances (the road being too bad for wheeled carriers) and evacuated to IIIrd Corps M.D.S.,direct.

8.   Light Sections of all C.F.A's were ~~xxxxxxxx~~ advanced to a point abreast of me at Divisional Report Centre and parked off the road. Their situation was indicated to O's C, C.F.A's who were with Brigade Head Quarters and discrettion given to each to move forward his own Unit if occasion demanded, reporting destination to me,

While on the other hand I had determined to use the combined Units, or such portions of them as remained, as circumstances dictated. All Motor Ambulances were retained at the point (R.9.b.8.8.) and were under my orders.

9. Communication between O's C, C.F.A.'s and Divisional Report Centre was well maintained. All casualties with the exception of a proportion of those incurred during the charge of a Squadron of the Fort Garry Horse and which could not be brought off owing to an enemy Counter-attack were recovered and evacuated through Infantry Advanced Dressing Stations. No ~~Canadian~~ Cavalry Field Ambulance of the Division opened under the circumstances though all were in a position to move forward and do so if conditions had necessitated it.

10. Casualties are as under;-

    British Officer Died of Wounds.....1.
    British Officers Wounded.............6.
    British Other ranks:- Killed........7.
                             Wounded.......37.
                             Missing.......56.

(sd) A.J.MACNAB.
Colonel.I.M.S.
A.D.M.S.,5th Cavalry Division.

24-11-17.

U.D.H. I. 2d Cav. Div.

"Medical" Volume XXXVII
Army Form C. 2118.

WAR DIARY / INTELLIGENCE SUMMARY

Wk 21st Dec 1917

NZMR ScCav Division

Place	Date	Hour	Summary of Events and Information	Remarks and references to Appendices
R.S.a. Two Trees West of EPEHY	21st Dec		No. 3 Brigade of the Division have been engaged. Ambulance Post in the exploded Sunken Road W. of BOSCAGNE E. of Rail. Hrs hit. Shell. See End Rifle in hospital in the re-capture of GOUZEAUCOURT by Rt. Edward's Horse and Canadian Bde - L.S.H. Macbrien in the attack on VILLERS GUISLANS Cavalrie Bde. Casualties shift evacuated by Ambulance Bearer posts. the flying between Regd. Aid Posts + front-line Ambulance wagons comet with removal to supply – the troops set up, worked admirably. Mr. Herron of MILNSTCH. A. under the Personal Direction Capt. F.R. NASSARD MC Commander in the absence of Major E.A.C. MATTHEWS VHS. I.M.S. on leave. Pati new covered 40 kilometres each in 24 hours + were indefatigable. Evacuation was to NEUVECOURT. Were dift for lectures See beds C.F.A. Speed on Advd Dressing Station in pneumonia visited by an My Ambulance in the morning on arrival of	

Army Form C. 2118.

WAR DIARY
or
INTELLIGENCE SUMMARY.
(Erase heading not required.)

Place	Date	Hour	Summary of Events and Information	Remarks and references to Appendices
Villers Faucon R.S.C.	Dec 1		The hostile shelling the motor ambulance available. The M.O. moved up from VILLERS-FAUCON to HEUDICOURT. Evacuation from Z FINS by rail by car by rail road with wind.	
do	Dec 2		See War Diary intelligence W/T reserve. The H.Q. at JAQUELINE Copse moved South of N.E. of War Report Centre. Canadian Cav. Bde holding a line from BOIS GAUCHE L- VAUCHELLES FARM. Canadian Light Horse Div'l 1/4/28. moved from Gurlu to HEUDICOURT.	
LONGAVESNES	Dec 3rd		Re Division intertherun during the night 2/3 w. Reinforced by 1st Cavalry Division. See War Diary between LONGAVESNES and SAULCOURT. Ambulance at - VILLERS-FAUCON. C.F.A. on war Dute. H/Qrs at - LONGAVESNES.	
do	Dec 6th		Still Canadian sustained by the Division and in position.	

WAR DIARY
INTELLIGENCE SUMMARY

Army Form C. 2118.

Place	Date	Hour	Summary of Events and Information	Remarks and references to Appendices
LONGAVESNES	6		**Killed.** British Officers 8, British Other Ranks 22, Indian Other Ranks 18. TOTAL 48. **Wounded.** British Officers 14, Indian Officers 4, British Other Ranks 120, Indian Other Ranks 87. 225. **Missing.** British Other Ranks 12, Indian Other Ranks 6. 18	
"	7		Ambulance Rate occupied Support line 4-12 trenches down vacated Rate H/Qrs. + the Advanced Dressing Stn. of MHOW C.F.A at HEUDICOURT.	
MONCHY LA CACHE	8		The Division moved South 14¾ to 61 MONCHY LA CACHE. See War Diary in RUIRE-COURCELLES area, AMBALA Bde i/c CARTENY area, Canadian Bde en-ROISEE. Th Gd. consist of a tourism party from the Division being employed in the defense on the line JEANCOURT - NESBECOURT - TEMPLEUX-LE- GUERARD, Canadian C.F.A at ROISEL with open a connection Communical Station.	

1577 Wt.W10791/1773 500,000 1/15 D. D. & L. A.D.S.S./Forms/C. 2118.

Place	Date	Hour	Summary of Events and Information	Remarks and references to Appendices
MONCHY LA GACHE	Aug 9		As November 2 a hasty examination of his division no crew of Franz Josef are reported and a further amount of similar chiefly empties to Canadian Rifle. Early Sept 2. unearthed my provisional divisions is much by the Division are being taken. So far no reports, prevalence of Lice have been reported cargo from one unit – the German Column R.C.H.A Bde. The Council Spies & Escort Spies have been attended, & a wing to the communication can — 2 – 8. Reporting habits— Reports white management, & to the working habits Service Arms guarantee action Sanitaire arrangements fermante, & dispo— Arrangements mit.l Open a Hospital at COURCELLES pour reception with of Sci Inst & Arnold Rifle. See bunk G.F.A with open fire. MAIN G.F.A. win arrears June from Rifle	
"		10"	The event of the Canadian Rifle moving to LE MESNIL area MN G.F.A win find the personnel for the compressors & Evacuations	

Army Form C. 2118.

WAR DIARY
INTELLIGENCE SUMMARY.
(Erase heading not required.)

Place	Date	Hour	Summary of Events and Information	Remarks and references to Appendices
MUNCHY LA GACHE	10th	10"	p.m. — In the event of this being necessary 6 staff horses will be received from Army Corps, and will be required. When L. form from this Regn. sections C.E.A. etc. are suitably arr... & train Courts is again in existence as a Regts. more etc. At schemes 2 Bdes Commanders when received from training in camp to Division have required to report details the time.	
		11"	Hardest weather change to hardness report. Division in progress of leaves guards by County Artry 8 days p. horse to Col. Murdoch G.O.C. yesterday evening. Orders having been issued that the division is to be held in readiness to reinforce & support the line in the event of HEBUTERNE, FONCQUEVILLERS... Orders have been issued to C.P.O. that in the event O.O.S. will move with their Brigades & report to G.O.C. 21-11 Bns & Cy. the C.O.R. section standing fast in the fields.	

O.C. Flanning Lt. Col. 11us

Army Form C. 2118.

WAR DIARY
or
INTELLIGENCE SUMMARY.
(Erase heading not required.)

Instructions regarding War Diaries and Intelligence Summaries are contained in F. S. Regs., Part II. and the Staff Manual respectively. Title pages will be prepared in manuscript.

Place	Date	Hour	Summary of Events and Information	Remarks and references to Appendices
MONCHY LAGACHE	3/12/17		The division has been in billets since Saturday, and not engaged in actual operations. A working party of 350 men from each Brigade in turn is being sent out daily each under C.R.E. 24 Div. Since 18th they work at roads from about 5 p.m. return back to their billets about midnight. Arrangements have been made to feed & rest rest Sup: and separate Retention Stations will the party and there is an A.D.S. and Regimental aid for in Clev Aide who has been detailed to receive any casualties that may have occurred. No Battn. strength party returns to town. Officer Bros slightly wounded. No news regarding the wounded party of Mederson transfer the line in the vicinity of HERBECOURT TEMPLECOURT Runs been cancelled by the orders issued on 28.[?] whereby the Division is in readiness to return at eight hours notice, on request to hold the line from the Riv OMIGNON & about 1000 yds South of TEMPLECOURT. Further reports to be at the disposal of 5 C.C. Divisional withdrawn, and the 6 No in Division. O.A. Return of Field Ambulances will accompany their Brigades and Fort Section will attend first wound the party A.D.M.S. the Division has been detailed moved into Monrguest works Quartier. The scheme for Divisional A/drew trips where no change and the 469 Standard Railway Effort for being. [?]	

1577 Wt. W10791/1773 500,000 1/15 D. D. & L. A.D.S.S./Forms/C. 2118.

WAR DIARY

INTELLIGENCE SUMMARY

Army Form C. 2118.

Place	Date	Hour	Summary of Events and Information	Remarks and references to Appendices
RENNY LAGACH	cont^d 31.12.17		Sanitary arrangements We also deficient as all as the washing of men's clothing. The following Casualties amongst M.O.'s have occurred. Lt. T. H. NORONHA J.M.S. evacuated sick on 13.12.17 Capt. W. M. S. BURNEY R.A.M.C. transferred to Command Depôt 14 K.D. amb. on 27.12.17 Capt. D. A. MURRAY R.A.M.C. transferred England on 23.12.17 Reinforcement received Capt. J. E. McCULLOUGH R.A.M.C. The weather has been very cold, (Hard frost and snow) for the last fortnight & inspite withstowe regarding the prevention of Trench feet has been circulated to all concerned officers and instruction regarding its prevention have been carried out by the Div. Sanytaire the injured Convalescent C.R. to Secunderoine C.C.L. in support of the treatment given. A complete rest station for British Sick and a rest station for Indian M.T.S. as also an Indian Sick treatment Centre is in existence. Since the opening of light Duty Coy. Capt. R. Y. FAGAN R.A.M.C. has been attached to v.v.D.S. of the Division A.H. Heming Lt. Col. R.A.M.C.	

Army Form C. 2118.

WAR DIARY / INTELLIGENCE SUMMARY

15th [?] XXXIII [?]
(Erase heading not required.)

Place	Date	Hour	Summary of Events and Information	Remarks and references to Appendices
MONCHY LAGACHE	1/1/18		Major C.F.A. Stewart to Headquarters Cairo on 1st Feb. and exchanges etc. etc. 4th Division Cav General departs at St Omer for Boulogne & Italian Arch [?] to H & S Squadrons Rehem not ready. Treating all Indians & Secunderabad 2nd Cavalry [?]. Secunderabad Rules. Capt. R.J. Jagan to O. in C. had been appointed D.O. to the 5th Cav Division. Reported 27th December 1917.	
	5/1/18		Orders for the dismounted division to take over the right sector of the line at present held by 3rd Dismounted Division were received on 3rd inst. The staff of the division was to take over the duties as staff of dismounted division. Assignments were made for Rehem & to Rehain the 7 Cav Hd. Qrs & take over dismounting duties at VADENCOURT & JEANCOURT. But on 11th orders cancelling this were again received yesterday that 4th Indian Regiment will to 5 Cav Brs, were ordered to Egypt & the 5 Cav Hd. Ambulances when the Portud personnel of 2 our were approved collected conference of C in C & Mr. S. at C in C's office on 2nd & 3rd. D.D.M.S has pointed out the desirability of arranging during course for the [...]	None. 5th Cav Smith [signature]

WAR DIARY
INTELLIGENCE SUMMARY.

Army Form C. 2118.

Place	Date	Hour	Summary of Events and Information	Remarks and references to Appendices

MONCHY LA GACHE 14th — Quiet bathing & draining Man. & Laundry facilities. Men sweating have been brought to notice of the Division. Also the bath wagon has been ordered by him to work the scheme. In the rear 1 Indian in this division is about 40 evacuated & the rest. This is due to overcrowding of latrines etc & with such cooties. Patrols working is not high about 40. Yr weather has been very warm, think have feet now the beginning of the month, but this has been a slow will result probably in ten days. Steve Feeney 'again today.

Colonel A.I. MACNAB returned from leave. A L Murray takes his returning to duties. A Lieut Lee Irwin.

15th — Lt.Col. A.N. FLEMING D.S.O. proceeded on I month leave next known has received of the afforestation department to EGYPT. Indian Cavalry Regts. of the 4, 5 & 7. Cavalry Division — Details including 3 complete 2nd Amb... lancers & 2 C.F.A. Non British including to representation have been notes in writing. (Copy attached) to the effect that

1577 Wt.W10791/1773 500,000 1/15 D.D.&L. A.D.S.S./Forms/C. 2118.

WAR DIARY
or
INTELLIGENCE SUMMARY.

Army Form C. 2118.

Place	Date	Hour	Summary of Events and Information	Remarks and references to Appendices
MONCHY LA CACHE	12		inspection Matrons in Personnel can be made without nivation & breakdown of the efficiency of their units. There are no intervals of brigades of companies - they should be to in every team of two types, who in respect personnel transport & equipment. References in Downs L. D.A. and Cavalry Corps for rates represent, above, & must - in L- by this move into the horses, troops probably be required to Advances in restitution to times gone. These were known or received & whether it would be attacked to - while limbers A.S. wagons for A.S. troops in a proportion to 3 G.S. trans for every 2 of the other Cavalry M-3 km of the two Divisions nearly been recipients of Immediate-Revent Amongst these were Lt S. DUTT late M.C. 8 A.F.C. of MHOW C.F.A. Indian	
"				

WAR DIARY

INTELLIGENCE SUMMARY.

(Erase heading not required.)

Place	Date	Hour	Summary of Events and Information	Remarks and references to Appendices
MUNCHY	19"		A. Virginia Serra [?] returned to 4 members of Regt.	
"	21"		Stephen Freeman V.J.F. & 18th Lancers for Scheme review	
			Inspected lines of Royal Canadian Dragoons	
"	22"		Inspected Canadian C.F.A.	
"	23"		Conference at office of D.D.M.S Cavalry Corps	
"	24"		Orders received by G.O.C. Cavalry Division visited over a security for the Divn. 4", 5" & 6" Canadian hi- Regt. 3	
			Infty Gde each of Cherbourg-Shepth of visited 4[?] Regts 13th Can Div 11- BOUVINCOURT	
			taking over Army A.Arnt Arrangements Services for division Arrangements then 3 together	
"	25"		Cavalry divns army started	
			ONC received for hunts to [?] divn L- withdrawn	
			to area surrounding by 3rd Cav divn - DOMART- EN-	
			PONTHIEU. Visited D.D.M.S Cavalry Corps	
"	26		General medical Arrangements - Post hunts	

WAR DIARY
INTELLIGENCE SUMMARY.
(Erase heading not required.)

Army Form C. 2118.

Place	Date	Hour	Summary of Events and Information	Remarks and references to Appendices
MONCHY	26th		[illegible] Division on [illegible] and Rest Area. [illegible] attached	
BOUVINCOURT	27th		AAD Announces Division moved to BOUVINCOURT; assumed duties of ADMS district Bertincourt 10 am relieving Lt.Col. C. MACKENZIE RAMC. Sent. DADMS — Capt. R.F. FAGAN RAMC — [illegible] help Reference to Aid Posts in Centre Right-Sector.	
	28th		Visited Advanced Dressing Stn. VADENCOURT. DADMS L. see Reg'l Aid Posts in L2 Subsector	
	29th		4th. DADMS L — see Advanced Dressing Stn. Rally Post & R.A.P. in Centre Sector between WARLICOURT & VILLERET. [illegible] Canadian Cav. Bde.	
	30th		[illegible] Inspected recently M.T. Convoy C.F.A. Conference [illegible] — Corps H Q D	

WAR DIARY
INTELLIGENCE SUMMARY
(Erase heading not required.)

Army Form C. 2118.

Place	Date	Hour	Summary of Events and Information	Remarks and references to Appendices
BOUVIGNY	30		[illegible handwritten entry]	

SECRET.

5th CAVALRY DIVISION.

OPERATION ORDER (MEDICAL) No.14.

A.D.M.S.
5TH
CAVALRY DIVISION.
No......
Date......

Copy No......... 15

Reference Map,
1/20,000.

24th January 1918.

1.   With reference to 5th Cavalry Division Operation Order No.30, dated 24th January 1918 the following Medical Personnel, transport, and Equipment is at the disposal of each Dismounted Brigade who will please issue the necessary instructions to all concerned except to the Field Ambulances and Sanitary Section which are receiving orders direct.:-

AMBALA DISMOUNTED BRIGADE.

Medical Officer:-	Captain.J.J.WAGNER.R.A.M.C.
Orderly for duty with M.O.:-	1 from 8th Hussars.
R.A.M.C., for water duties:-	2 from 8th Hussars.
Sub-Assistant Surgeon.:-	from 9th Hodson's Horse.
Ward Orderly:-	from 18th Lancers.
Stretcher Bearers.:-24.:-	8 from 8th Hussars.
	8 from 9th Hodson's Horse.
	8 from 18th Lancers.
For Sanitary duties:-	2.B.O.R., from 8th Hussars.
	2.I.O.R., from Sanitary Section, for each Indian Regiment.
Batman for M.O.:-	1 from 8th Hussars.

TRANSPORT.

One half L.G.S. wagon for Medical Equipment.

EQUIPMENT.

1.Pair Field Medical Panniers:-	from M.O.,8th Hussars.
2.Field Medical Companions:-	1 from M.O.,8th Hussars.
	1, from M.O.,9th Hodson's Horse.
2.Field Surgical Haversacks:-	1 from M.O.,8th Hussars.
	1 from M.O.,9th Hodson's Horse.
2.Haversacks, Shell Dressings.:-	1 from M.O.,8th Hussars.
	1.from M.O.9th Hodson's Horse.
12 Field Stretchers:-	from Mhow I.C.F.A.
50.Ammonia Capsules.	
1.Gallon Whale Oil.	
5 Lbs. Oxford Grease.	
5.lbs. Oxford Powder.	

CANADIAN DISMOUNTED BRIGADE.

Medical Officers:-	Captain.W.J.E.MINGIE.C.A.M.C.
	Captain.J.C.McCULLOUGH.C.A.M.C.
Orderlies for duty with M.O's.:-	1 from R.C.Dragoons.
	1 from L.S.Horse.
C.A.M.C., for water duties:-	2 from F.G.Horse.
Sanitary Orderlies:-	2 per Regiment.
Stretcher Bearers:-24.:-	8 from R.C.Dragoons.
	8 from L.S.Horse.
	8 from F.G.Horse.

TRANSPORT.

Two half L.G.S.,Wagons for Medical Equipment.

EQUIPMENT............

EQUIPMENT.

2.Pair Field Medical Panniers:-   1 from M.O.,R.C.Dragoons.
                                       1 from M.O., L.S.Horse.
2.Field Medical Companions.:-   ------do------
2.Field Surgical Haversacks.:-   ------do------
2.Haversacks, Shell Dressings.:-   ------do------
12.Field Stretchers.:-   from Canadian C.F.A.
50.Ammonia Capsules.
1.Gallon Whale Oil.
5.Lbs Oxford Grease.
5.Lbs. Oxford Powder.

SECUNDERABAD DISMOUNTED BRIGADE.

Medical Officer:-   Captain.J.N.CRUICKSHANK.RAMC.
Orderly for M.O.:-   1 from 7th Dragoon Guards.
Sub-Assistant Surgeon:-   from 34th Poona Horse.
Ward Orderly:-   from 20th Deccan Horse.
R.A.M.C., for water duties:- 2 from 7th Dragoon Guards.
Sanitary Orderlies:-   2.B.O.R., from 7th Dragoon Guards.
                          2.I.O.R., from Sanitary Section
                          for each Indian Regiment.
Stretcher Bearers:-24.:- 8 from 7th Dragoon Guards.
                          8 from 20th Deccan Horse.
                          8 from 34th Poona Horse.
Batman for M.O.,   1 from 7th Dragoon Guards.

Transport and Equipment as for Ambala Dismounted Brigade, the 12 Field Stretchers to be found by Mhow I.C.F.A.
The Lance Pattern Regimental Stretcher will not be taken into the line.

2. O.C.,MHOW.I.C.F.A., will take over the Advanced Dressing Station of both Sub-Sectors at JEANCOURT and VADENCOURT respectively, with his Head Quarters at BIHECOURT, relieving No.3.C.F.A. Advance Parties to report at JEANCOURT and VADENCOURT by noon 26th inst. Relief to be completed by midnight JANUARY 26th/27th. Two Motor Ambulances and one Cyclist will be posted at each Advanced Dressing Station, remainder of Ambulance transport will be at BIHECOURT and available as occasion demands.

3. O.C.,Canadian C.F.A., will place 1 Medical Officer and 2. other ranks at the disposal of O.C.,Mhow I.C.F.A., as a temporary measure. They will report at TERTRY noon January 26th.

4. The Regimental Aid Posts for Right Sub-Sector is in Bookers Quarry R.11.a.8.4. Forward Aid Posts at R.6.a.central, R.4.d.7.9., and M.7.b.0.6. are available when necessary.
The Regimental Aid Posts for Left Sub-Sector are the Quarry at L.28.c.5.8., R.5.a.7.5. and at L.33d.3.9. which last will be considered as a Relay Post for the Regimental Aid Post at R.5.a.7.5.

5. The transport of all wounded unable to walk is by hand under Regimental arrangements from the line to R.A.P., thence by Bearer parties with wheeled carriers to the Advanced Dressing Stations.

6. All wounded will be sent to the Corps Main Dressing Station BERNES except urgent cases requiring immediate surgical attention e.g., wounds of head and abdomen which will be evacuated to TINCOURT in the case of British ranks, or to PERONNE in the case of Indians direct.

7. British sick will be sent to No.7.C.F.A., at POEUILLY, Indian sick to St.CREN.

8.................

8. Canadian and Sec'bad C.F.A's will stand fast and be prepared to move Westward with Mounted portion of the Division. Till further orders Sec'bad C.F.A., will collect and evacuate British and Indian sick of Sec'bad Brigade and Indian sick of Ambala Brigade. Canadian C.F.A., will collect and evacuate sick of Canadian Brigade, and Divisional Troops, and British sick of Ambala Brigade.

9. Particulars regarding all sources of water supply and the amount of chlorination necessary will be issued later.

10. ACKNOWLEDGE (C.F.A's and Sanitary Section only)

Macnab
Colonel, I.M.S.
A.D.M.S., 5th Cavalry Division.

24-1-18.

```
Copy No.1..................Sec'bad Cavalry Brigade.
  "  No.2..................Ambala      "        "
  "  No.3..................Canadian    "        "
  "  No.4..................Mhow I.C.F.A.
  "  No.5..................Sec'bad I.C.F.A.
  "  No.6..................Canadian C.F.A.
  "  No.7..................Sanitary Section.
  "  No.8..................C.R.H.A.
  "  No.9..................5th Cavalry Division "G".
  "  No.10.................5th Cavalry Division "Q".
  "  No.11.................A.D.M.S., 1st Cavalry Division.
  "  No.12.................A.D.M.S., 4th Cavalry Division.
  "  No.13.................D.M.S., Fifth Army.
  "  No.14.................D.D.M.S., Cavalry Corps.
  "  No.15-17..............War Diary.
```

SECRET.

5th CAVALRY DIVISION.

OPERATION ORDER (MEDICAL) No.15.

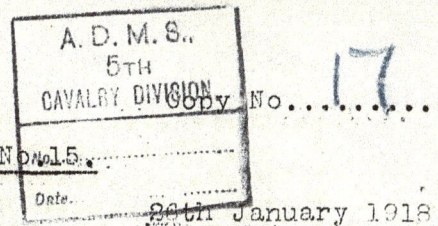

Copy No. 17

Date. 26th January 1918.

Reference Map.
1/100,000.

1. In accordance with 5th Cavalry Division Operation Order No.51, dated January 26th 1918 that portion of the Division not employed in the line will move to the 3rd Cavalry Division area by Brigades on January 28th and subsequent dates.

2. Canadian and Sec'bad Cavalry Field Ambulances will march and billet under orders of the Brigade to which they are attached.

3. O.C., Sec'bad C.F.A., will place 1 horsed and 1 motor ambulance at the disposal of Captain.J.G.N.FIRTH.R.A.M.C., who will be S.M.O., Ambala Cavalry Brigade during the march. On the conclusion of which he will rejoin his Unit and be relieved by Lieut.W.A.REARDON.I.M.S.,

4. 5th Cavalry Divisional Sanitary Section will remain under orders of A.D.M.S., Dismounted Divisions until further notice.

5. While on the line of march sick will be evacuated as follows:-

EAST of VILLERS-BRETONNEUX:-
British sick:- Light cases to Cavalry Corps Rest Station, CAPPY. Officers, and other cases, except Infectious and Special cases to No.42 Stationary Hospital. AMIENS.
Infectious and Special cases to No.41. Stationary Hospital. GAILLY-CERISY.

Indian sick:- To Lucknow C.C.S. PERONNE-LA-CHAPELETTE.

WEST of VILLERS-BRETONNEUX:-
British sick to No.42 Stationary Hospital. AMIENS.
Infectious and Special cases as above.

Indian sick:- As above.

All cases on the line of march will be shown as "Transfers".

6. On arrival in the new area Lieut-Colonel.A.C.RANKIN.C.A.M.C., O.C., Canadian C.F.A., will assume the duties of Senior Medical Officer of the Division in addition to his own.

7. O.C., Canadian C.F.A., will open on arrival and will collect and admit sick of Canadian Cavalry Brigade, British sick of Ambala Cavalry Brigade and of Divisional Troops.

8. O.C., Sec'bad C.F.A., will also open, and will collect and recieve British and Indian sick of his own Brigade and also Indian sick of Ambala Cavalry Brigade.

9. After arrival in the new area British sick may be evacuated either to ABBEVILLE or AMIENS. Infectious cases, and Special cases, to No.41. Stationary Hospital. GAILLY-CERISY. Orders regarding evacuation of Indian sick will issue later.

10. Rear Report Centre will open at DOMART-EN-PONTHIEU at 12 Noon January 30th.

11. ACKNOWLEDGE. (Canadian & Sec'bad C.F.A's & Sanitary Sec: only)

Colonel.I.M.S.
A.D.M.S., 5th Cavalry Division.

26-1-18.

P.T.O............

```
Copy No.1-3............C.B.A's.
  "  No.4-6............Brigades.
  "  No.7..............Sanitary Section.
  "  No.8..............Capt.Firth.RAMC.
  "  No.9..............Lieut.Reardon.I.M.S.
  "  No.10.............D.M.S.,Fifth Army.
  "  No.11.............D.D.M.S.,Cav Corps.
  "  No.12.............Col.Adams. 20th Horse.
  "  No.13.............A.D.M.S.,3rd Cav Div.
  "  No.14.............A.D.M.S.,4th Cav Div.
  "  No.15.............5th Cav Div "G".
  "  No.16.............5th Cav Div "Q".
  "  No.17-19..........War Diary.
```

Statement showing number of admissions to Cavalry Field Ambulances, evacuations, transfers to Rest Stations, and number returned to duty during the month of January 1918.

	Admissions.	Evacuations.	Rest Stations.	To duty.	Remarks.
British.	(a) 370	(b) 148	(c) 139	(d) 85	(a) Includes 188 Canadians (b) " 74 " (c) " 78 " (d) " 35 "
Indians.	117	81	12	24	
Totals.	487	227	151	109	

Average daily strength of Division for the month:- British. 5887. Indians. 3307.

Statement showing number of cases of Preventable Diseases admitted to Cavalry Field Ambulances during the month of January 1918.

	British.	Indian.
DIARRHOEA.	5	2
SCABIES.	74 *	18
VENEREAL.	8	-
PNEUMONIA (Lobar)	-	1
MUMPS.	-	1
MINOR FEVERS;P.U.O.,etc.	57	15

* Includes 53 Canadians.

Secunderabad Ind. Cav. F.A.

Jan. 1918

www.ingramcontent.com/pod-product-compliance
Lightning Source LLC
Chambersburg PA
CBHW081539160426
43191CB00011B/1795